Designing and Implementing Semantic Data Layers

Dave Wells

Technics Publications
SEDONA, ARIZONA

TECHNICS PUBLICATIONS

115 Linda Vista, Sedona, AZ 86336 USA
https://www.TechnicsPub.com

Edited by Steve Hoberman
Cover design by Lorena Molinari

First Printing 2026

ISBN, print ed. 9798898161620
ISBN, Kindle ed. 9798898161637
ISBN, PDF ed. 9798898161644

Contents

Introduction 1

Chapter 1: The Meaning of Data 5
- Ontology and Taxonomy 6
- What Is Data Semantics? 9
- The Roles of Semantics in Data Management 10
- Why Semantics Is Needed Now 18

Chapter 2: What Is a Semantic Data Layer? 21
- Five Types of Semantic Data Layers 23
- Architectural Components of a Semantic Layer 28
- Implementation Components of a Semantic Layer 31

Chapter 3: Building a Semantic Data Model 35
- Semantic Data Modeling Begins with the Domain 35
- Knowledge Graphs 36
- Property Graphs 38
- The Semantic Data Modeling Process 39
- Ontology: Concepts, Relationships, and Definitions 46
- Properties in the Semantic Model 49
- Taxonomy Analysis 51
- Putting it All Together 56

Chapter 4: Semantic Layers in Data Architecture 61
- The Semantic Model as Architectural Anchor 61
- Semantic Layers in Architectural Context 62
- The Enterprise Layer as Architectural Foundation 63
- Domain Layers and Operational Data Management 64
- Domain Layers and Data Products 66
- Integration Layers: From ETL Coding to Semantic Mapping 67
- The Enrichment Layer: Preserving Meaning Through Analytics Pipelines 68
- Consumption Layers and Consumer Interfaces 69
- From Implicit to Explicit Meaning 70

Chapter 5: Implementing Semantic Data Layers 71
- From Architecture to Software 71
- Implementation Approaches 72
- Four Implementation Patterns 77
- Which Patterns Fit Where? 81
- Choosing Patterns Based on Need 83

Semantic Layer Components in Operation 84
Semantic Layer Engineering 87

Chapter 6: Planning and Evolving Semantic Architecture 89
Four Architectural Patterns 90
Where to Start 99
How Much Coverage Is Needed? 102
Sequencing the Work 103
The Parallel Path: Semantic Modeling and Architectural Evolution 104
Designing for Evolution 105
Principles for Your Architectural Journey 107

Chapter 7: Putting It into Practice 109
Applying the Principles 109
Assessing the Current State 112
Best Practices for Data Semantics 116
The Broader Significance 120
Where to Begin 121

Index 123

Introduction

This book grew out of something I see happen frequently: data management has a meaning problem. Organizations invest heavily in data infrastructure (data lakes, warehouses, pipelines, platforms) but fail to recognize semantic layers as critical infrastructure. Yet questions that should be easy to answer remain stubbornly hard. What does "active customer" mean? Why do two reports produce different revenue numbers? How do we combine data from the CRM and billing systems without losing something in translation?

These are not technical problems. They are semantic problems. The data exists. The technical infrastructure works. What is missing is shared, explicit, governed meaning: a common understanding of what the data represents, documented in a form that systems and people can rely on.

Semantics, ontology, taxonomy, and semantic modeling are not new ideas. But they have typically been applied as point solutions: a data dictionary here, a business glossary there, a metadata layer on top of a BI tool. What's missing is a coherent architectural framework that brings the pieces together, shows how they relate to each other, and gives architects and engineers something they can actually build and operate. That is the goal of this book.

The book is organized as a journey from first principles to practical application. It starts with what semantics means and why it matters in data management. It moves through the five types of semantic data layers and the modeling and design techniques used to build them. From there, it covers implementation approaches (APIs, data products, data contracts, data virtualization, and schema registries) and the four implementation patterns that determine how semantic meaning is realized in software. The final chapters address architecture and practice: how semantic layers fit into and evolve across four architectural patterns, from loosely connected data environments to AI-ready infrastructure, how to plan that evolution, and how to get started.

AI has sharpened the urgency of all of this. Large language models and agentic systems are only as reliable as the context in which they operate. A knowledge graph that captures your organization's concepts, relationships, and definitions is not just good data management. It is an essential part of what makes AI outputs explainable and trustworthy. The organizations that invest in semantic infrastructure now are also investing in AI readiness, whether they realize it or not.

This book is written for data architects, engineers, and leaders who are responsible for making data consistent, trustworthy, and useful across their organizations. It is also written for an emerging role that I call Semantic Layer Engineer: the practitioner who combines technical fluency, modeling precision, and organizational sensibility to build the infrastructure of shared meaning.

Data is now abundant in every organization. Meaning is not. The gap between the two is where friction and frustration are amplified, analytical projects stall, AI outputs become unreliable, and integration work quietly accumulates technical debt. Closing that gap is architectural work, and it is among the most consequential work in data management today. This book is a guide to doing that work.

CHAPTER ONE

The Meaning of Data

"I once shot an elephant in my pajamas.
How he got in my pajamas I'll never know."

Groucho Marx

Semantics is the study of meaning. Specifically, it focuses on the meaning of words, symbols, and expressions, and how that meaning is understood in context. The Groucho Marx joke is funny precisely because it exploits a semantic ambiguity. The sentence is grammatically correct. It parses just fine. But the phrase "in my pajamas" can attach to either the speaker or the elephant, and that ambiguity produces an absurd second sentence.

Syntax tells you whether a sentence is well-formed. Semantics tells you what it means. You can have perfect syntax and broken semantics. In data management, this is not a theoretical concern. It happens constantly.

Syntax is about form. Semantics is about meaning.

When a database column is named customer_id, the database management system does not care what that means. It cares whether the value is the right data type and satisfies any defined constraints. Meaning is not a DBMS job. It is a human's job. And in large organizations, with data distributed across dozens or hundreds of systems built by different teams over years or decades, the humans responsible for meaning often have different points of view, or have moved on, taking their knowledge with them.

We apply semantics to data to make the meaning explicit, consistent, and persistent.

Ontology and Taxonomy

Two foundational concepts appear throughout this book: ontology and taxonomy. They come from philosophy and biology respectively, but in data management they have precise and practical meanings.

An ontology is a formal description of knowledge as a set of concepts and the relationships among those concepts. An ontology for a business domain identifies the real-world things that exist in that domain (customers, orders, products, payments, etc.) and describes how they relate to one another. A customer places an order. An order generates an invoice. An invoice requires payment. Those relationships, stated formally and accompanied by controlled vocabulary and explicit definitions, constitute an ontology.

A taxonomy is a system of hierarchical classification used to group things based on similarity and difference. The classic example is the biological taxonomy: kingdom, phylum, class, order, family, genus, species. In business data, a taxonomy might be a product category hierarchy, a classification of customer types, or the set of valid states an order can be in.

The distinction between the two is important. An ontology is about existence and relationships: what things are and how they connect. A taxonomy is about classification: how things are grouped and ordered hierarchically. You need both to build a complete semantic model. The ontology gives you the backbone of concepts and connections. Taxonomy adds depth: the sub-types, categories, and classifications that give the model richness and precision.

We need both an ontology and a taxonomy.
The ontology provides the connections,
and the taxonomy provides the classification.

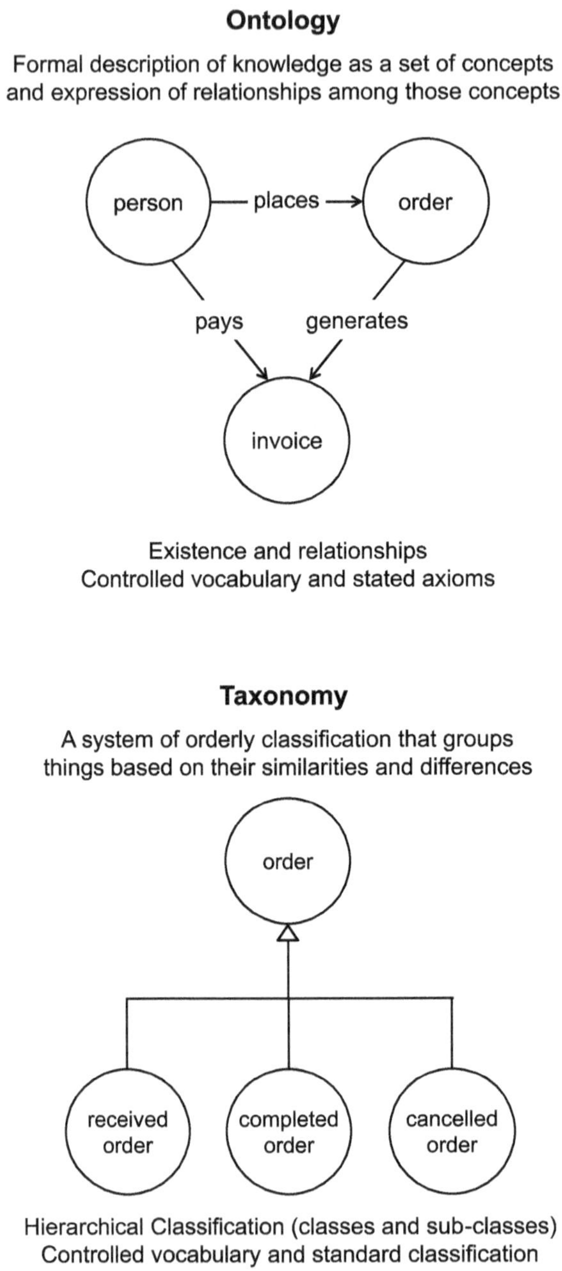

Figure 1: Ontology and Taxonomy.

What Is Data Semantics?

Data semantics focuses on how a data object represents a concept or object in the real world. That is the core question: not "What is in this field?" but "What real-world thing does this field represent?"

> *Semantics, applied to data, is the discipline of making meaning explicit, consistent, and durable.*

Consider a field called customer_id in a database. What does it actually mean? Is it the identifier for the person who placed the order? The identifier for the person who received the invoice? The identifier for the person who made the payment? In different systems, the same name might mean different things. Or the same concept might have different names in different systems: purchaser_id, billing_contact_id, account_holder_id. All of these might identify the same underlying concept, the person who has a business relationship with the company, or they might each refer to something subtly different.

Data semantics makes that meaning explicit and consistent. It establishes a shared definition: here is what we mean by "customer." Here is how a customer relates to a rental. Here is how renter_id in system A maps to customer_id in system B, because both refer to the same real-world concept. Without data semantics, organizations rely on tribal knowledge. The people who built the system know what it means. New team members must ask around. Analysts build reports based on assumptions. When two systems are integrated, someone discovers that "customer" means different things in each, and a difficult and expensive reconciliation follows.

Data semantics is the discipline of solving that problem systematically and sustainably.

The Roles of Semantics in Data Management

Semantics touches nearly every major activity in data management, which is part of why it is so easy to underestimate. Its value is not concentrated in a single use case. It is distributed across the work organizations do every day to manage, integrate, govern, and use data.

The most fundamental role is **establishing shared meaning**: consistent definitions for data elements across systems, teams, and uses. When each group develops its own vocabulary, the organization accumulates incompatible interpretations, and the cost of reconciling them grows with every new system and every new team. Revenue means different things to Finance, Sales, and Marketing. Customer means different things to CRM, Billing, and Service.

Shared meaning depends on **stable naming and identity**. If customer_id in one system and account_number in another both refer to the same person, that equivalence needs to be established explicitly and maintained. When it is left implicit, integration requires human intervention every time something changes, and something is always changing.

Stable identity is what makes **reliable data integration** possible. Most integration work is semantic work: figuring out what data in one system means in terms that another system understands. When those mappings are explicit and governed, integration becomes a managed capability. When they live in code and tribal knowledge, integration is fragile and the cost of maintenance grows steadily over time.

Integration, done well, leads to **data interoperability**: the ongoing ability of systems and platforms to exchange and interpret data consistently. Interoperability is not a one-time achievement. It is a durable capability that must survive system changes, team changes, and architectural evolution. Semantic layers are what make it sustainable.

Semantics drives **reduced ambiguity and misinterpretation** that cause data to be misused. Every time a consumer has to guess what a field means, there is a chance they will guess wrong. Explicit definitions, classification structures, and interpretation rules replace those guesses with documented understanding.

Clear, unambiguous meaning supports **guided data access and consumption**: a semantic layer translates between the business vocabulary people use and the physical structures that store the data, making self-service access practical and reliable. Clarity of meaning brings **increased data reuse**. When a definition is documented and shared, it can be applied across many analyses without being reinvented each time. When each use case develops its own interpretation, those interpretations diverge in ways that are costly to detect and correct.

Semantics is a cornerstone of **governance and stewardship**. Defining ownership, applying rules, and enforcing appropriate use all require the ability to describe data precisely and consistently. A semantic layer provides that foundation. Semantics is the way to **preserve data meaning through change**. Systems evolve. Schemas are refactored. Data moves from one platform to another. In each of these transitions, meaning that lives only in code or in people's heads tends to be lost. A semantic layer treats meaning as a portable artifact, independent of the physical infrastructure that carries it.

Ultimately, semantics is the foundation for **trust and confidence** in data. Users trust data when they understand what it represents. That understanding has to be accessible not just to the engineers who built the system, but to every person who needs to use it. Trust in data is not a sentiment. It is a capability, and semantics is how you build it.

The Messy World of Enterprise Data Management

A typical enterprise data architecture often looks like something that has been patched together and added to for many years without a specific plan. Operational systems are a collection of legacy, ERP, and SaaS applications, each with local data structures, naming, and definitions. The systems are typically interconnected through a tangle of point-to-point data feeds with meaning embedded in application code at every connection point. Operational data integration is attempted through operational data stores and master data management (MDM) systems. The operational systems are further connected to analytics infrastructure through ETL processes that copy data into data warehouses and data lakes. Data meanings and translations are embedded in the ETL code. The subtleties of local meanings and data encodings are often lost in data transformations. AI data preparation acquires data from operational sources, data warehouses, and data lakes, and further transforms the data, compounding semantic disparity.

This is a fragile data management approach burdened with a high level of technical debt. Any change to data meaning, encoding, or database schema is likely to affect many data flows, including point-to-point feeds and ETL processes. Organizations rarely have complete inventory and reliable documentation for all of these connections. Impact analysis is difficult and time-consuming, with a high risk of side effects and unintended consequences when change occurs.

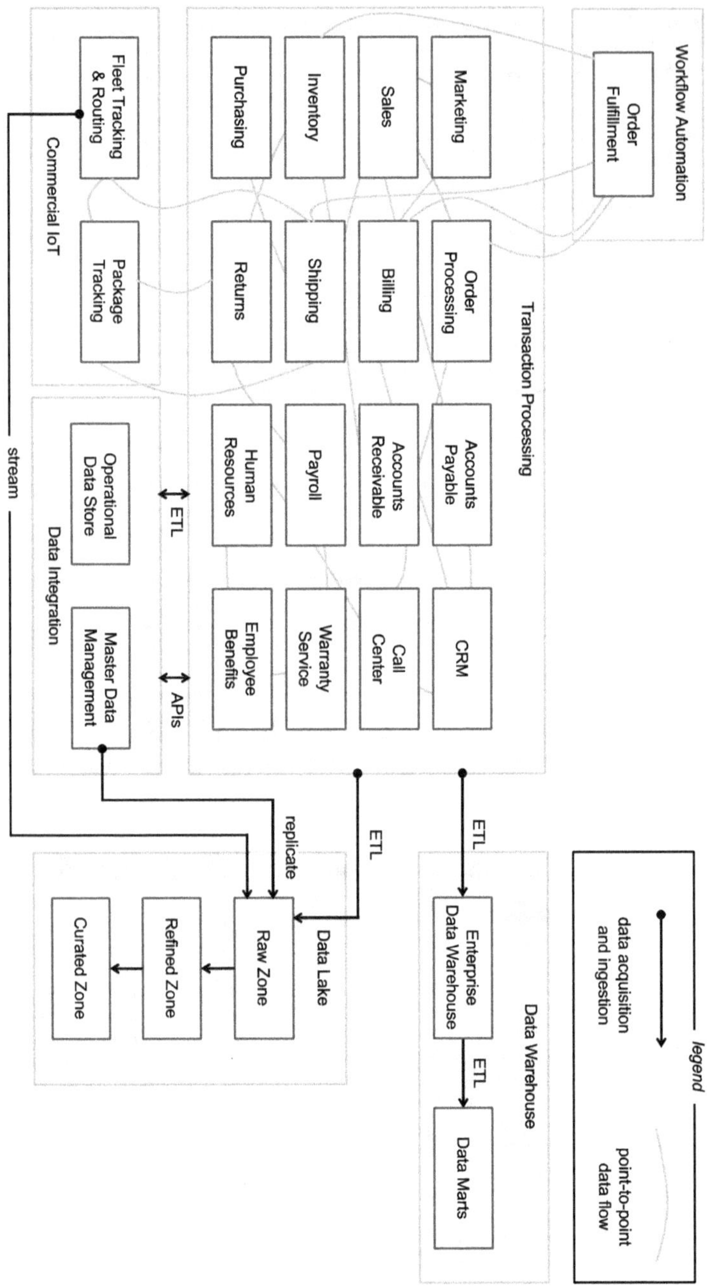

Figure 2: The Messy World of Enterprise Data Management

The Cost of Copy-Based Integration

Most enterprise data architectures move data by copying it. An ETL job reads from one place and writes to another. A replication process keeps two databases in sync. A data pipeline loads data into a lake and then refines it through successive stages. Each copy is a potential point of semantic drift where meaning changes, degrades, or is entirely lost.

Data copies are costly. Every copy requires maintenance. Every transformation embeds semantic assumptions. Lineage becomes difficult to trace. Data quality problems propagate and multiply. Privacy and compliance risks multiply with each copy of sensitive data. Scalability suffers as the number of copies grows.

The deeper problem is technical debt. Each copy, each transformation, and each point-to-point connection represents a commitment that must be honored indefinitely. When a source system changes its schema, every downstream copy and transformation that depends on it requires rework.

When meaning shifts (for example, when "active customer" is redefined or a new product category is added), that change must be propagated manually through every pipeline and integration process that works with the data. Over time, the cost of maintaining existing data infrastructure crowds out the capacity to build new things. Most of the data engineering effort is spent keeping existing pipelines running.

Semantic data layers offer a different approach. Instead of copying data and relying on code to preserve meaning through the transformation, they make meaning explicit and portable. Meaning can travel with data and be applied at points of access, without requiring that data be physically moved to another location.

The Path from Data to Value

Even when data is technically available, it is often practically inaccessible. Getting from raw data to useful insight requires five steps: finding the data, accessing it, understanding it, preparing it, and analyzing it. Semantics plays a role at every step.

Finding data depends on knowing what exists and what it represents. Without documented meaning, data catalogs and search tools return results that consumers cannot evaluate. You can find a table named customer_transactions, but it isn't useful without knowing what it contains and how well the content matches what you need.

Accessing data requires more than a working query. Business people should be able to work in business terms. This means capabilities such as asking for "active customers in the Northeast" without knowing or caring how that translates to physical tables, columns, and join conditions. A semantic layer bridges that gap, exposing data through business vocabulary that reflects how the business thinks, not how the data is physically structured. Semantic query and self-service access become practical when the meaning of the data is explicit and the translation to physical storage is handled under the hood.

Understanding data is where semantics has the most direct impact. Knowing what a field represents, what its valid values are, and how a metric is calculated are all questions of meaning. In the absence of documented, consistent definitions, data consumers must guess at meaning. And they guess incorrectly more often than they realize.

Preparing data for use requires reconciling it with other data. That reconciliation is semantic work: mapping fields, resolving naming differences, aligning definitions across sources. Without a semantic foundation, every preparation effort starts from scratch.

Analyzing data correctly depends on correct and consistent definitions. When definitions vary across analyses, the same data produces different results. An analysis of customer retention may show different conclusions depending on how "customer" and "active" are defined. Conclusions drawn from inconsistent definitions and misunderstood data often lead to less-than-ideal business decisions. Semantics is the basis for shared, stable definitions that support reality-based conclusions.

Why Semantics Is Needed Now

The case for data semantics is not new. But the urgency has grown because the environments where data lives are significantly more complex than they were a decade ago, and the tolerance for ambiguity has dropped substantially.

Today's data environments have six challenges that make implied meaning elusive and unsustainable: Data Sprawl, Data Disparity, Data Silos, Data Friction, Global Data Complexity, and Data Chaos.

A decade ago, an organization might manage data across a handful of core systems and data sources. Today, data sprawls across dozens or hundreds of cloud platforms, SaaS applications, IoT sensors, mobile apps, and third-party feeds.

Each system and data source has its own vocabulary, its own schema, and its own implicit definition of what "customer," "transaction," or "active" means. More sources lead to greater data disparity, more vocabularies, and greater difficulty in reconciling the differences. Governance programs that struggled to keep up a decade ago are now overwhelmed.

Organizational structure adds to the challenge. Sales has its CRM. Finance has its ERP. Operations has its supply chain systems. Each was designed for a singular purpose, with its own data model. Data silos are a natural consequence of specialization. But they create real costs when the organization needs to reason across them, and those costs compound as the number of systems grows.

The result is data friction: the accumulated effort required to find, access, understand, and prepare data for use. It shows up as time spent trying to make sense of what a field means, reconciling reports that show different numbers for the same metric, and building integration code that requires rework with every source system change. Every organization has it. Most have more of it than they realize.

For organizations operating across countries and regulatory jurisdictions, there is an additional layer. The meaning of "address," "name," and "tax identifier" varies across legal systems and cultures. Semantics gives you the vocabulary to document that variation and navigate it consistently.

Left unaddressed, these challenges accumulate. Data sprawl grows. Silos deepen. Disparity widens. Friction builds. The result is data chaos: an environment where meaning is implicit, inconsistent, and elusive. As data chaos compounds, the cost of not having a semantic foundation becomes impossible to ignore.

Chapter Two

What Is a Semantic Data Layer?

"The beginning of wisdom is the definition of terms."

Attributed to Socrates

A semantic data layer is a data management concept that separates data meaning from data structure, allowing heterogeneous systems to exchange and interpret data consistently. That separation of meaning from structure is the central idea. Physical databases have schemas. Schemas have tables, columns, data types, and constraints. Those are structural concerns. What those structures represent (what real-world things and what relationships they capture) is a semantic concern. Separating the real-world perspective from the structural view gains an important degree of freedom.

When meaning is embedded in structure, meaning changes when structure changes. A column gets renamed; anyone who knew what the old name meant now has to re-learn. A table gets split; the logic that once was used to query a single table now needs to understand two tables and their relationships. A system gets replaced; all the semantic knowledge encoded in the old schema must be painstakingly reconstructed in the new one.

When meaning is separated from structure and expressed in a semantic layer independent of any particular schema, it can persist through structural changes. The semantic model remains stable while the physical systems beneath it evolve.

Look at semantic data layers through three lenses:
Purpose: *to define and stabilize meaning.*
Architecture: *to mediate between sources and consumers.*
Implementation: *software to operationalize mediation.*

It is useful to think about semantic data layers from three different perspectives: purpose, architecture, and implementation.

From a purpose perspective, a semantic data layer's job is to define concepts, relationships, and interpretation rules for data independently of underlying systems and schemas. The layer provides a stable semantic model that connects data from multiple sources to common concepts—concepts with agreed-upon definitions that do not change when a source system is updated.

From an architecture perspective, a semantic data layer is a component that sits between data sources and data consumers. It receives requests in semantic terms using the vocabulary of business concepts, and it translates them into queries against physical data structures. It receives data from those structures and returns it in semantic terms. The architectural role is mediation: bridging the gap between how data is stored and how it is understood.

From an implementation perspective, a semantic data layer is software that operationalizes semantic models by mediating between physical data sources and consuming applications. It stores and manages the semantic model. It maintains mappings between semantic concepts and physical data structures. It applies rules and context. And it exposes the resulting semantic capabilities through interfaces that consumers can use.

Five Types of Semantic Data Layers

Not all semantic layers are the same. Different parts of a data architecture need different kinds of semantic support, and a mature semantic architecture contains multiple layers serving a variety of purposes. Five common types of semantic data layers meet a diverse set of data management needs.

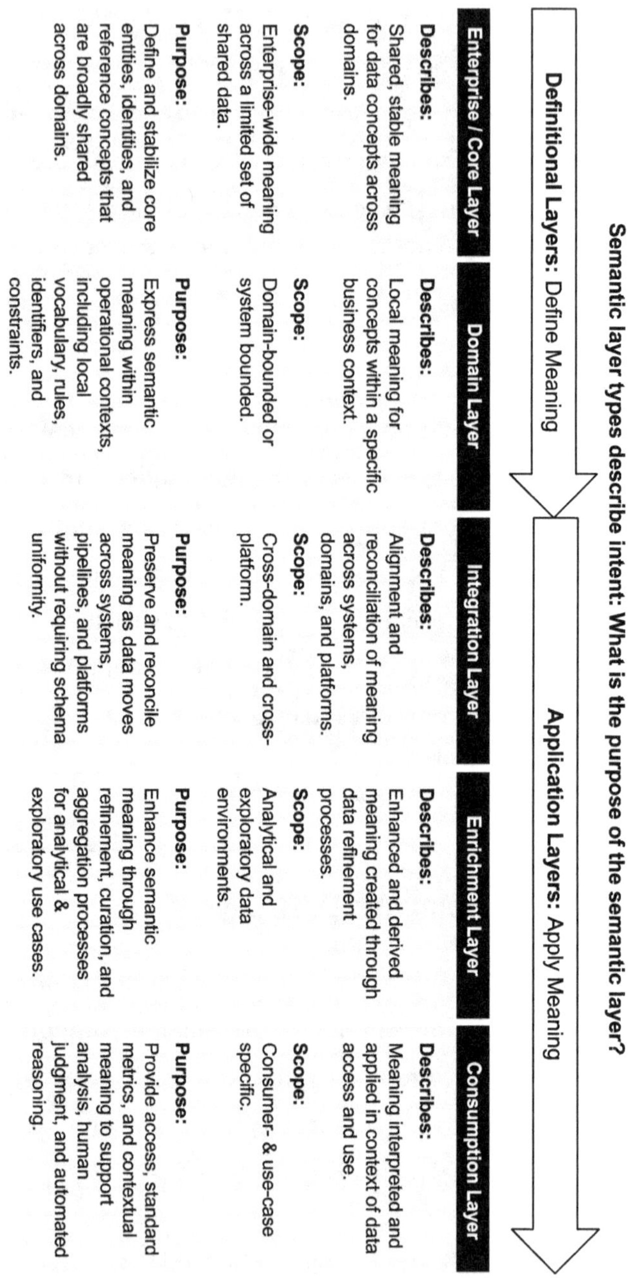

Figure 3: Five Kinds of Semantic Data Layers.

The Enterprise or Core Layer

The enterprise or core layer describes shared, stable meaning for data concepts across the entire organization. Its scope is deliberately narrow: it covers the limited set of data concepts that are truly shared across domains. The concepts defined in the enterprise layer are similar to the entities of master data management (MDM): customer, product, account, employee, etc. These are the concepts that need to have common and consistent meaning across all business areas. MDM and the enterprise semantic layer address the same underlying problem in different ways. MDM manages stored data using deduplication and golden record techniques. The enterprise semantic layer manages the definitions that make those records interpretable.

The enterprise layer defines the core concepts that every part of the business must agree on:
customers, products, accounts, etc.
If that sounds like master data, it should. The enterprise semantic layer and MDM solve related problems. They work best when they work together.

The enterprise layer's purpose is to define and stabilize core entities, identities, and reference concepts. It does not try to cover everything; it covers what matters most broadly. A well-designed enterprise layer changes slowly because the fundamental business concepts it describes are stable. Customers and products, for example, do not reinvent themselves every fiscal year.

Domain Layers

Domain layers describe local meaning for concepts within a specific business context. Functional domains such as sales, finance, orders, and customer service typically have local data dialects. Within each domain, data has localized vocabulary, rules, and interpretations that may not apply outside that domain.

Domain layers serve two purposes: They make local meaning explicit within the domain, which supports interpretation across the people and systems in that domain. And they provide a governed interface between the domain and other data management domains. This enables data interoperability without requiring all domains to use identical schemas.

Integration Layers

Integration layers describe alignment and reconciliation of meaning across systems, domains, and platforms. The purpose is to preserve and translate meaning as data moves across boundaries without requiring every system to adopt a uniform schema.

This type of semantic data layer shifts integration from a process of physical transformation to one of mediated meanings. Instead of writing ETL code with embedded data transformation logic, semantic mappings specify how concepts in one system or domain map to those in another. An integration layer makes those mappings explicit, versioned, and reusable.

The Enrichment Layer

The enrichment layer describes enhanced and derived meaning: the meaning created when raw data is refined, aggregated, and curated through analytical and computational processes. Its scope spans analytical environments, exploratory data analysis, AI data preparation, and feature engineering.

Derived data without documented meaning is an answer without a question. An enrichment layer captures the decisions behind the math.

The key problem that the enrichment layer solves is, "When you compute a derived metric or engineered feature, what does it mean?" A thirty-day rolling average of transaction value sounds self-explanatory, but what is a "transaction" in this context? Does it include canceled orders? Is it revenue or gross margin? Is it calculated per customer, per region, or across the entire business? The same questions apply to AI features: what data was used, how was it transformed, and what real-world concept does the resulting variable represent? The enrichment layer captures those decisions explicitly, so that derived meaning is consistent, documented, and reusable across the analyses, models, and applications that depend on it.

Consumption Layers

The consumption layers describe meaning as it is interpreted and applied in the context of specific data access and use. Different consumers need the same underlying data presented in ways that align with their specific purposes. A business intelligence dashboard for executives needs aggregated metrics in familiar business terms. An operational API needs real-time data with strong transactional semantics. An AI model needs precisely defined, consistently prepared data, with the meaning of each input variable explicitly defined and stable. An agentic application needs data it can reason over, which requires meaning to be expressed in terms the agent can interpret and act on.

The semantic foundation remains stable.
A consumption layer adapts it to the context language of the data consumer.

Consumption layers provide context-specific interpretation on top of the more stable layers. It is the most volatile of the five types because new use cases and consumer types create additional consumption layers. It builds on stable foundations, so new consumption needs can benefit from established meaning without having to reconstruct it from scratch.

Architectural Components of a Semantic Layer

Understanding what a semantic layer does requires understanding what it is made of. At the architectural level, three components work together. The semantic model defines the concepts, relationships, properties, classifications, and definitions that give data its meaning. Semantic context captures the settings in which that meaning is applied, because the same concept can mean different things in different situations. Interpretation rules govern how meaning is enforced in practice, through constraints, derivations, and logic.

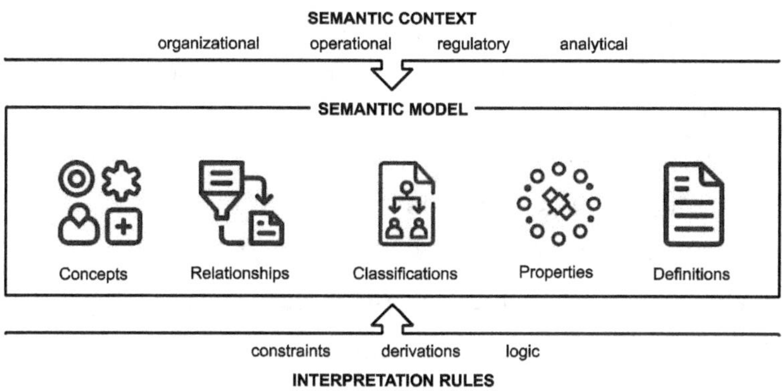

Figure 4: Semantic Layer Architecture Components.

The semantic model is the heart of a semantic data layer. It contains five kinds of content:

- **Concepts are the things the model describes**: The business entities, processes, and ideas that the data represents. Customer, rental, vehicle, payment, and location are all concepts.
- **Relationships describe how concepts connect**: A customer contracts a rental, a rental provides a vehicle, a payment satisfies a rental obligation.
- **Properties are the facts about concepts and relationships**: A customer has a name, a license number, a birthdate. A rental has a status, a vehicle cost, a start date.

- **Classifications organize concepts and properties into hierarchical structures**: Rental statuses are reserved, active, completed, or terminated. Location types are airport, hotel, suburban, or rural.
- **Definitions are the written explanations of every term in the model**: They are precise statements of meaning that distinguish a semantic model from a mere diagram.

Semantic context captures the settings in which meaning is applied: organizational context (which business unit, which domain), operational context (which process, which transaction), regulatory context (which jurisdiction, which compliance regime), and analytical context (which use case, which metric definition). Context matters because meaning can vary. "Customer" in a regulatory context might carry legal obligations that "customer" in an analytics context does not. Semantic context makes those variations visible and explicit. That's a big improvement over leaving them hidden and embedded in code. **Interpretation rules** govern how semantic meaning is applied in practice. They include constraints (what must be true, what cannot be true), derivations (how calculated values are computed from raw data), and logic (rules for classification, inference, and semantic translation).

Together, the semantic model, semantic context, and interpretation rules constitute a complete semantic layer at the architectural level. The model defines what things mean. Context specifies when and where those definitions apply. Rules govern how meaning is enforced and applied.

Implementation Components of a Semantic Layer

Architectural components describe what a semantic layer does. Implementation components describe the software needed to make it work. Each component has data, metadata, and processing sub-components. Data sub-components store the content the component manages. Metadata sub-components capture the descriptions, definitions, rules, and context that give that content meaning. Processing sub-components execute the operations that put both to work. This three-part structure repeats across all six components because the same fundamental needs apply everywhere: something to store, something to describe it, and something to act on it. The separation is intentional. Keeping data, metadata, and processing distinct makes each easier to manage, evolve, and replace independently.

Semantic model management stores and manages the semantic model: the concepts, relationships, classifications, properties, and definitions. This might be implemented as a graph database, metadata repository, knowledge graph platform, or specialized semantic store. Whatever the technology, it needs to persist the model, support versioning, and make the model query-friendly.

Semantic context and rule management manage contextual interpretations, constraints, and rules. It is where the context-sensitive behavior of the semantic layer is captured: the rules that specify how meaning varies across organizational contexts, regulatory environments, and use cases.

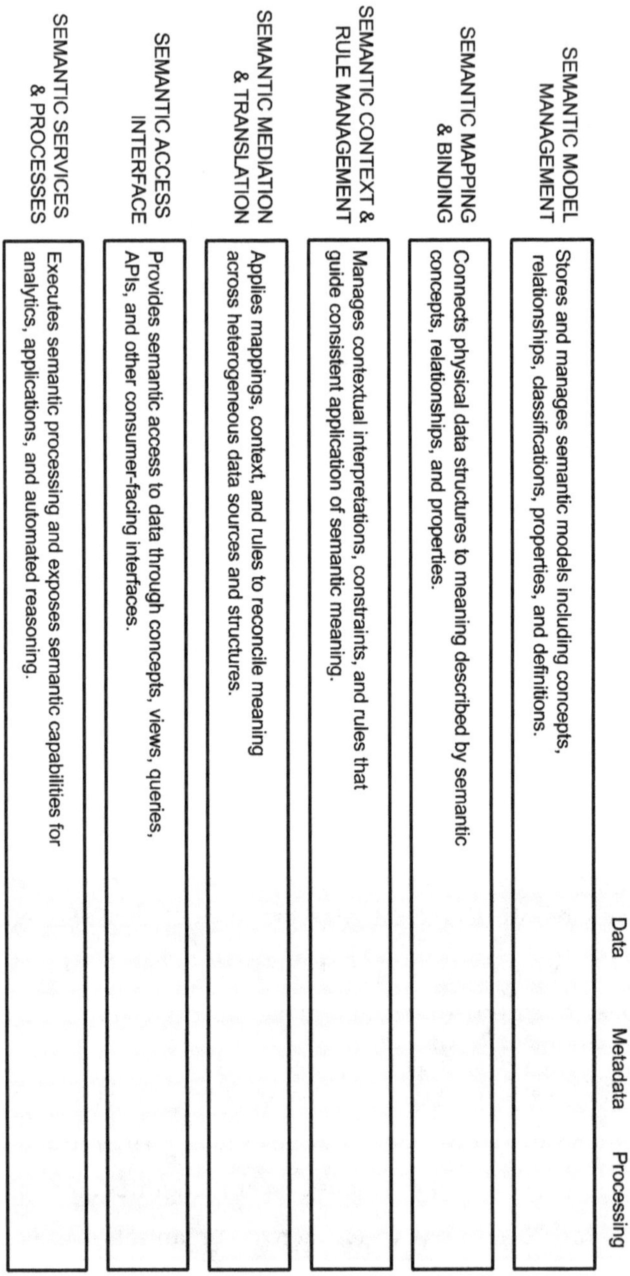

Figure 5: Semantic Layer Implementation Components.

Semantic mapping and binding connect physical data structures to the meanings described in the semantic model. A mapping states that the customer_id column in the ORDERS table of the CRM database corresponds to the customer concept in the semantic model. Binding makes those mappings active at runtime — when a query requests customer data, the binding directs it to the appropriate physical sources.

Semantic mediation and translation apply mappings and rules to reconcile meaning across heterogeneous sources. When data from two systems needs to be combined, this component handles the semantic reconciliation. It translates local terminology into shared concepts, resolves identity mismatches, and applies the rules that govern how data from different sources should be interpreted together.

Semantic services and processes execute semantic processing and expose semantic capabilities to consumers. This is the runtime layer that handles semantic queries, executes translations, applies classifications, calculates derived metrics, and makes semantic layer capabilities available through well-defined interfaces.

Semantic access interface is the consumer-facing surface of the semantic layer. It provides semantic queries, views, APIs, and other interfaces that enable consumers to request data in business terms. The interface shields consumers from the complexities of physical data, presenting a stable, semantically consistent view regardless of what is happening in the underlying physical systems.

Collectively, these components implement a data supply chain with explicit semantic management at every step. A consumer requests data in semantic terms. The request arrives at the semantic access interface. The semantic model provides the vocabulary to interpret the request. Semantic services execute the appropriate processing. Semantic mappings direct the execution to the right physical sources. Data flows back through the semantic layer, semantically enriched with meaning from the model to the consumer.

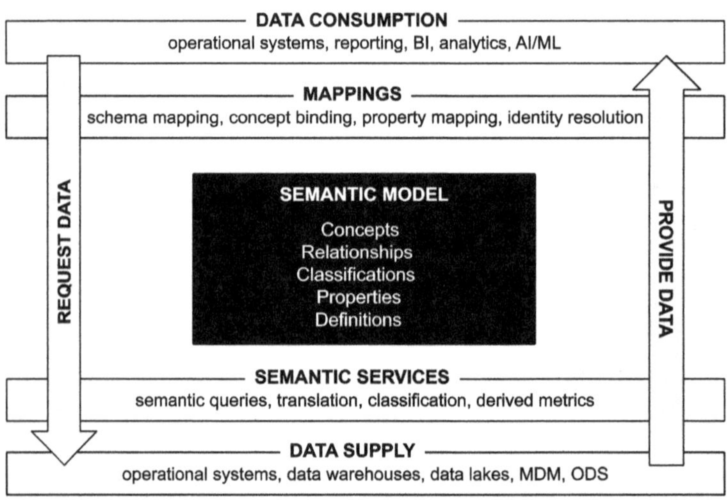

Figure 6: Connecting Consumers to Data.

This flow has an important implication: consumers do not need to know where the data lives or how it is structured. They need to know the business concepts. The semantic layer handles the rest. That transparency is not just a convenience. It is what makes the semantic layer a durable architectural component. As physical systems change, the semantic interface remains stable. Consumers are insulated from churn in the physical world.

CHAPTER THREE

Building a Semantic Data Model

"All models are wrong, but some are useful."

George Box

Semantic Data Modeling Begins with the Domain

Semantic data interoperability begins with semantic data modeling. Before you can build a semantic layer, you need a model that documents a precise description of the concepts, relationships, and properties in the domain, expressed in a form that is both rigorous and understandable.

The modeling approach described in this chapter uses graph models: knowledge graphs and property graphs. Graph models are well-suited to semantic modeling because they mirror the way humans naturally think about the world as things and relationships. They are also visually intuitive, which makes them effective communication tools for the conversations between data professionals and business stakeholders that good semantic modeling requires.

Throughout this chapter, the working example is vehicle rentals. The domain is easily understood, yet complex enough to illustrate the full range of modeling concepts. By the end of the chapter, you will have seen a step-by-step build of a semantic model.

Knowledge Graphs

The fundamental unit of a knowledge graph is the triple: subject, predicate, object. Every relationship in a knowledge graph is expressed as a triple: a simple assertion that can be read as a sentence. The subject does something (the predicate) to or with the object.

> *Every fact in a knowledge graph is a complete sentence: subject, predicate, object. The simplicity of triples makes knowledge graphs both expressive and composable.*

These three terms have both semantic and graph interpretations, and understanding both is useful. Semantically, the subject and object are concepts: the things the model describes. The predicate is a relationship: the named connection between two concepts. In graph terms, concepts are represented as nodes and relationships as edges. The subject is a node, the object is a node, and the predicate is the edge connecting them. Figure 7 illustrates this with a simple example from the vehicle rental domain.

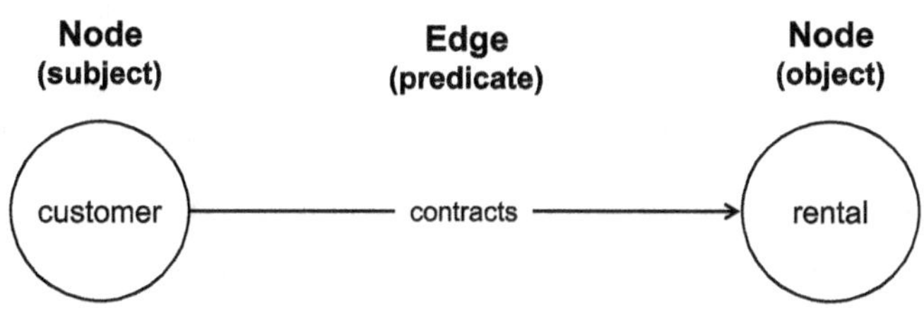

Figure 7: Knowledge Expressed as a Triple.

Customer is the subject node. Rental is the object node. Contracts is the predicate edge connecting them. The triple is a simple sentence: *Customer contracts rental.* That sentence asserts knowledge about a business relationship. This simple structure is surprisingly expressive. Knowledge about any domain can be represented as a collection of triples. Every triple is a complete, self-contained statement, so knowledge graphs are naturally composable: you can add new triples without disrupting the existing model. New concepts, new relationships, and new assertions fit in cleanly, because each triple stands on its own.

Property Graphs

Knowledge graphs describe structure: things and their relationships. Property graphs extend knowledge graphs by adding attributes, the properties of things and relationships, to both nodes and edges. The customer node in the graph has the following properties: customer id, first name, last name, driver license number, driver license state, and birthdate. Those properties capture the facts collected to identify and describe each customer. Similarly, the rental node has properties such as a rental id and cost information.

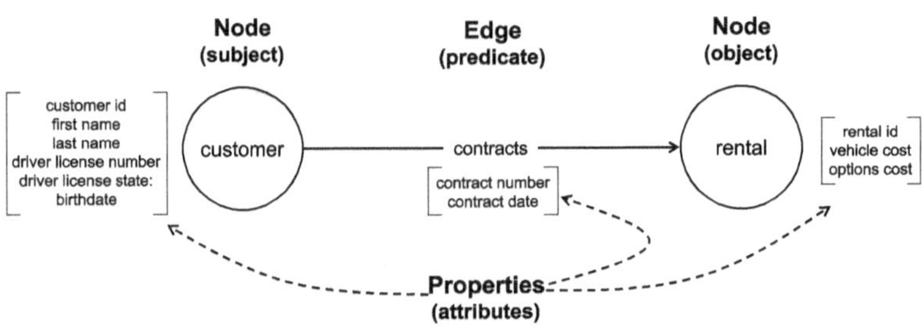

Figure 8: Extending from Knowledge Graph to Property Graph.

Edges can have properties too. The relationship between a customer and a rental (the act of contracting) has a contract number and a contract date. Those facts belong to the relationship, not to the customer or the rental independently. Property graphs give you the precision to make that distinction.

The Semantic Data Modeling Process

Building a semantic data model is an iterative process of analysis and refinement. Five analytical activities form the core process, supplemented by two analytical disciplines that run throughout.

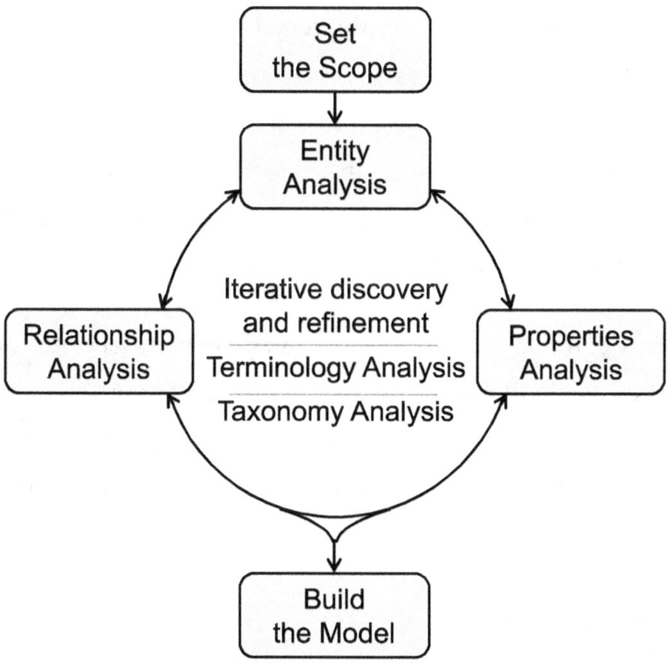

Figure 9: The Semantic Data Modeling Process.

Setting the Scope

Before modeling begins, describe the model's purpose, context, coverage, and boundaries:

- What domain are you modeling?
- What use cases will the model support?

- What is explicitly outside scope?

Semantic modeling begins with the domain, not with the data.

For the vehicle rental example, the scope is the rental transaction domain: what is involved in the rental lifecycle from reservation through return. Concepts such as customers, rentals, and vehicles are readily apparent and provide a good starting place. The model covers the rental lifecycle from reservation through return. Vehicle maintenance, employee management, and financial accounting are out of scope.

Scope definition seems obvious, but it matters enormously in practice. Without explicit boundaries, models may grow without limit. A focused model that covers its domain well and delivers value is far more useful than an ambitious model that never gets finished.

Entity Analysis

Entity analysis asks, "What are the real-world things that are represented as data?" These are the nouns of the domain. Look for the things that have independent existence, that we collect data about, that persist over time.

In the vehicle rental domain, five entities emerge from analysis: customer, rental, vehicle, payment, and location. Notice what is not on this list. There is no separate entity for driver. A driver is a customer in this model. There is no separate entity for transaction. Rental and payment are the transactions in the domain. They are distinctly different kinds of transactions. Each has its own properties and relationships. Cost is not an entity. Each rental has a single value for cost, so it is a fact about a rental and a subject of properties analysis.

Entity analysis requires judgment. Don't list everything that exists. Only include things that are significant enough to be first-class citizens of the model. Answer these three questions:

- Does this thing have an independent identity?
- Does it have properties of its own?
- Does it participate in one or more relationships?

If yes to all three, it is an entity. Model it as a node.

And don't attempt to create an exhaustive list of entities before moving to relationship analysis. Remember that this is an iterative process. When you look for entities, you'll discover relationships. When you examine relationships, you'll discover more entities.

Relationship Analysis

With only a few entities identified, sometimes as few as only two, it is natural to begin exploring relationships. Relationship analysis asks how these things are connected. With entities modeled as nodes, relationships become the edges of the knowledge graph. They represent the interactions, associations, and dependencies among entities.

Two practical guides help identify relationships. First, think in verbs. Ask, "What does a customer do?" A customer contracts a rental. A customer makes a payment. A customer operates a vehicle. The verbs give you the relationships. Second, examine directionality. Prefer active voice with the subject doing something to the object: "customer contracts rental" instead of "rental is contracted by customer." Active voice makes relationships more intuitive and avoids the ambiguity of the passive voice, which can obscure meaning.

For the vehicle rental domain, eight relationships emerge: customer contracts rental, rental provides vehicle, customer makes payment, rental requires payment, vehicle picked up at location, vehicle reserved at location, vehicle returned to location, and customer operates vehicle.

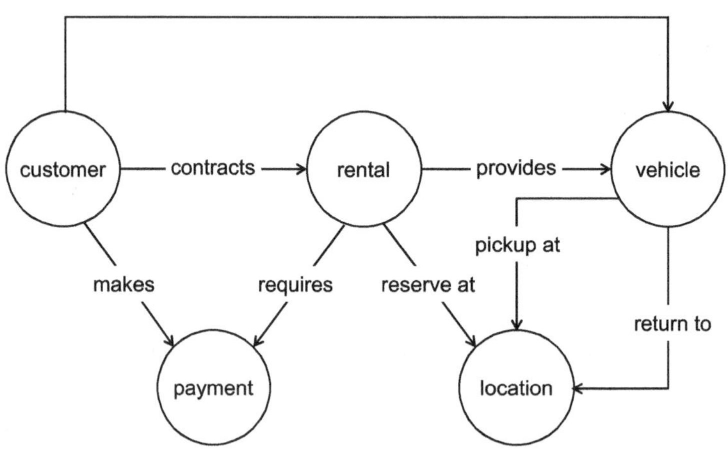

Figure 10: Vehicle Rental Knowledge Graph.

The customer-operates-vehicle relationship is less obvious than the others. It represents the period during which a customer has physical possession of and responsibility for a vehicle. This relationship matters for insurance, liability, and incident reporting. Good relationship analysis surfaces the less-visible connections that schemas rarely make explicit.

Properties Analysis

Properties analysis asks, "What facts are needed to identify and describe each entity, and what facts describe each relationship?" Note that for entities it makes sense to ask about identifying properties. Relationships are identifiable by the subject and object that they connect.

For the customer entity: customer id, first name, last name, driver's license number, driver's license state, and birthdate. For the rental entity: rental id, rental status, vehicle cost, options cost. For the vehicle entity: vehicle id, VIN, vehicle class, make, model, year, miles. For the payment entity: payment id, payment type, payment date, payment status, payment method, payment amount. For the location entity: location id, location name, location type, city, state. Of course, each of these entities is likely to have many more properties. But for illustration purposes in this book, we don't need to list all of them.

Edge properties capture facts about specific instances of relationships. The relationship between a rental and its pickup location includes properties for pickup date and time. The relationship between a rental and the return location has return date and return time properties.

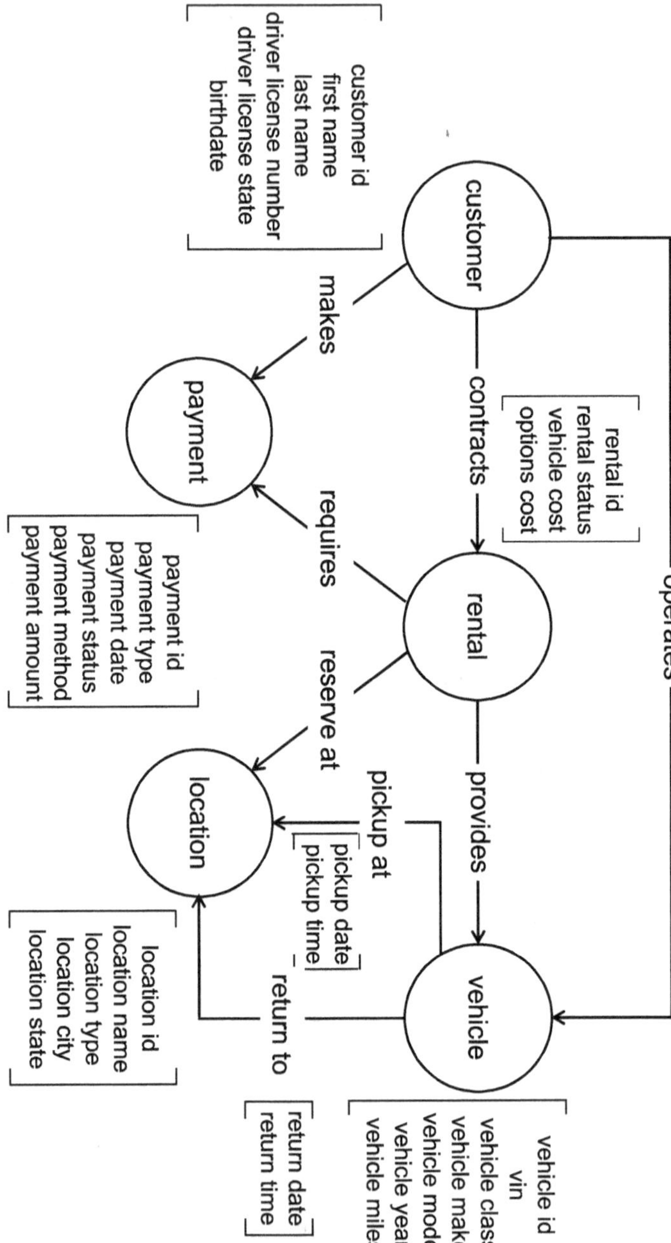

Figure 11: Vehicle Rental Property Graph.

Properties analysis is where semantic modeling engages most directly with actual data. You are asking:

- What data exists?
- What do these fields actually represent? And that inquiry often surfaces important ambiguities.
- What does "vehicle miles" mean? Is it total odometer reading, miles in the current rental, miles since last service, or something else?

Properties analysis forces precision that isn't visible in schemas.

Terminology Analysis

Terminology analysis is a cross-cutting activity that runs throughout the modeling process. The purpose is to surface and resolve the vocabulary of the domain. Perform terminology analysis with the goal of understanding the terms people use, what those terms mean, and how local terminology maps to standardized and controlled vocabulary.

The key questions:

- What terminology is used in this domain?
- What does each term mean specifically in the context of the domain that is being modeled?
- Which terms are local dialect: nicknames, abbreviations, or legacy names that persist?
- What should the standard term be?
- What is the standard definition?

Terminology analysis frequently reveals that the same word is used for different things in different parts of the organization, or that different words are used for the same thing. A "renter" in the reservations system might be the same concept as a "lessee" in the contract system and an "account holder" in billing. Identifying these overlaps is essential before mappings can be defined.

A model without definitions is only a diagram.
A model with definitions is a semantic artifact.

Every term that enters the semantic model needs a written definition. Not a one-liner, but a precise statement that eliminates reasonable ambiguity. This is one of the most time-consuming aspects of semantic modeling, and also one of the most valuable. The definitions transform a diagram into a semantic model.

Ontology: Concepts, Relationships, and Definitions

Entity analysis, relationship analysis, and terminology analysis produce ontology: a formal description of the domain as a set of concepts and the relationships among them, accompanied by controlled vocabulary and explicit definitions for every term in the model.

Figure 12 illustrates the ontology for the vehicle rental domain as a knowledge graph diagram. It contains five entities and eight relationships. The diagram is only the visual part of the ontology.

A useful semantic model includes definitions of all terms in the model, both nodes and edges.

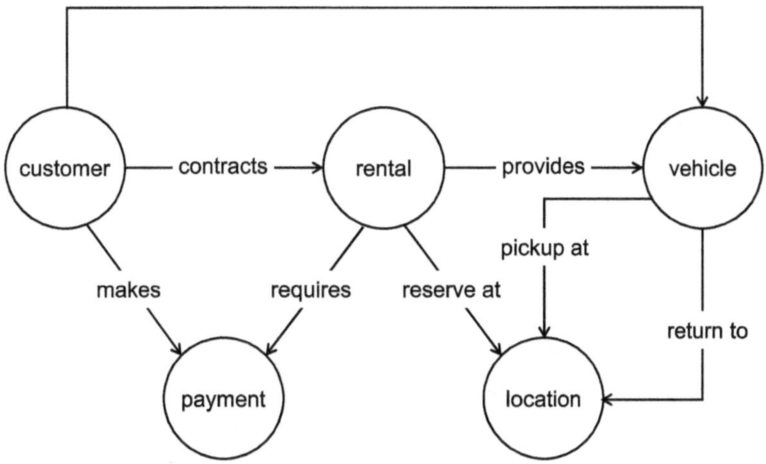

Figure 12: Vehicle Rental Ontology as a Knowledge Graph.

Customer	A customer is a person who has one or more agreements (current or past) to rent and/or operate vehicles owned by the company. Renters & authorized drivers are customers.
Rental	A rental is an agreement between the company and a customer that authorizes use of a specific vehicle for a period of time. Rental terms specify fees, constraints, and renter obligations.
Vehicle	A vehicle is a licensed and insured motor vehicle that is a unit in the rental fleet. Passenger vehicles, light trucks, and cargo vans are part of the fleet. Larger commercial vehicles are excluded.
Payment	A payment is a financial transaction submitted by a customer to compensate the company for rental fees, road tolls, fines, or other costs incurred in the course of renting and operating a vehicle.
Location	A location is a company facility at which vehicles are parked, serviced, and maintained. Vehicles are picked up from and returned to locations specified in rental agreements.

Contracts	Customer CONTRACTS Rental: A customer contracts a rental when they pick up a vehicle. A rental agreement describes the terms of the rental and is a legally binding contract.
Provides	Rental PROVIDES Vehicle: A rental provides one vehicle for use by a customer for an agreed-upon span of time, governed by terms expressed in a rental agreement.
Operates	Customer OPERATES Vehicle: A customer operating a rental vehicle is either the renter or an authorized driver. A driver who is not the renter is authorized only for the duration of the rental, must be a licensed driver, and must be age 25 or older.
Reserve at	Rental RESERVE AT Location: A rental reservation reserves a vehicle at a specific location. Each reservation specifies the location at which the vehicle is to be picked up.
Pickup at	Vehicle PICKUP AT Location: A vehicle is picked up at a company-operated rental facility. Reservations specify the location. Non-reserved rentals occur at a rental facility.
Return to	Vehicle RETURN TO Location: Vehicles are returned to company-operated rental facilities. The planned return location is agreed at time of pickup. Exceptions may occur with return to an unplanned location.
Requires	Rental REQUIRES Payment: Rentals require payment of vehicle and option fees as expressed in a rental agreement. Additional payments may be required for refueling, tolls, fines, and damages.
Makes	Customer MAKES Payment: Customers make payments for costs of vehicle rental including rental fees, option fees, damages, road and bridge tolls incurred, and parking fines incurred.

Notice the detail in the definitions. They are actually a combination of definition and description. The CUSTOMER definition explicitly includes authorized drivers, making it clear that customers extend beyond primary renters. The OPERATES relationship definition captures a business rule (the 25-year age requirement) that would never appear in a schema but is essential to fully understand the meaning of the relationship. This is the distinctive value of a semantic model:

> *A semantic model captures the business knowledge embedded in the domain (the rules, exceptions, and context-specific interpretations) and makes it explicit, durable, and accessible.*

Properties in the Semantic Model

Adding properties to the ontology produces a property graph that represents both the structure of the domain and the data collected to describe it. Properties analysis produces more than a list of fields; it is a semantically annotated list where every property is defined, constraints are documented, and any dependencies on other properties are noted.

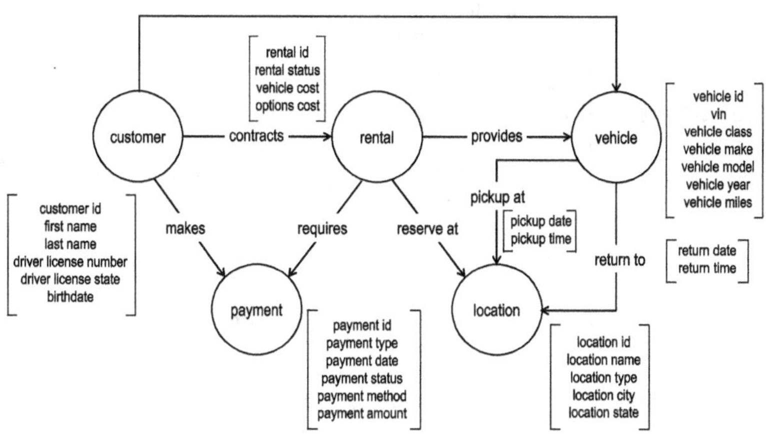

Figure 13: Vehicle Rental Semantic Model as a Property Graph.

Rental ID	An internally generated integer that is used to uniquely identify each instance of a rental agreement.
Rental Status	Indicates if a rental is reserved, active, completed, or terminated. Completed rentals end on the scheduled return date. Terminated rentals end due to abnormal incidents.
Vehicle Cost	The base fee for a vehicle for the term of the rental, excluding fees for optional items and services; also excluding charges for tolls, fines, damages, and other costs incurred by the renter.
Options Cost	The total dollar amount of charges for options selected by the renter. Options include fuel purchase, child seats, GPS navigation, and other add-ons.
Payment ID	An internally generated integer that is used to uniquely identify each payment transaction.
Payment Status	Describes the state of a payment as requested, received, or declined.
Vehicle Miles	The last recorded odometer reading at the time of vehicle return.
Location Type	Categorizes rental facilities as airport, hotel, suburban, and rural.
Driver License Number	The identifying number for a customer's driver license. Although called a number, it may be an alphanumeric value. The format of driver license number is determined by the issuing authority and varies by country and state.
Driver License State	Most frequently the US state that issued a customer's driver license. For licenses issued outside the US, country code is used in place of state abbreviation. Diplomatic and Dept. of State issued licenses are identified as USGOV
And 23 more property definitions, 5 entity definitions, and 8 relationship definitions	

Some properties require special attention. Consider driver license number. A developer encountering this field for the first time might reasonably assume it is a numeric field. In fact, a driver license number may be alphanumeric. Many US states and most countries use formats that include letters. Without a property definition that makes this explicit, a developer might create a numeric column and silently discard valid data.

The property definition also handles edge cases that schemas cannot easily express: for international licenses, the country code is used instead of the state abbreviation; diplomatic and US Department of State licenses are identified by a special code. These are the kinds of details that live in the heads of the most experienced team members. Capturing them in property definitions makes them permanent.

Taxonomy Analysis

Taxonomy analysis adds classification structure to a semantic model. It is not a separate step in the modeling process; it is woven throughout entity analysis, relationship analysis, and properties analysis. The language used to name and describe properties provides indicators of where taxonomy analysis may be needed. Look for words such as type, status, class, category, and kind. For properties using this language, ask what the defined values of each property are, and what each means. Then ask what is being classified: an entity, a relationship, or the values of a property.

Entity taxonomy classifies things. It identifies sub-classes of an entity. In the example here, we're looking at the rental entity, which has a property named rental status. The use of the term status indicates that we may classify rentals based on the states in which they exist. Taxonomy analysis finds that rentals may exist in any of four states: reserved, active, completed, or terminated.

Identifying entity subclasses is meaningful when any of the subclasses has unique properties or unique relationships that are not true for all of the subclasses.

Figure 14 illustrates the semantic model additions produced by taxonomy analysis of the rental entity. Each rental subclass has unique properties. A reserved rental has a reservation date, reservation method, and vehicle class code. When the renter picks up the vehicle, it becomes an active rental, with properties added to the record: vehicle ID, pickup time, pickup mileage, and pickup fuel level. When the vehicle is returned, the rental is completed. Vehicle ID is carried forward for completed rentals. Return time, return mileage, and return fuel level are added. When a rental ends due to an abnormal incident such as an accident or a legal issue, the rental is classified as terminated. A terminated rental adds properties for termination date, termination time, termination mileage, incident type, and incident location. Rental termination introduces a new entity, incident, which represents the abnormal event that ended the rental.

This last point is worth noting: taxonomy analysis sometimes surfaces new entities. The terminated rental subtype surfaces an incident as an entity not identified in earlier entity analysis. Iterative refinement is not a sign of poor analysis. It is the way that good semantic models are built through discovery and refinement.

Also worth noting is the need for further analysis of terminology. This example of taxonomy analysis introduces four subtypes, eighteen properties, one additional entity, and one new relationship into the model. That's twenty-four new terms that need to be defined and described.

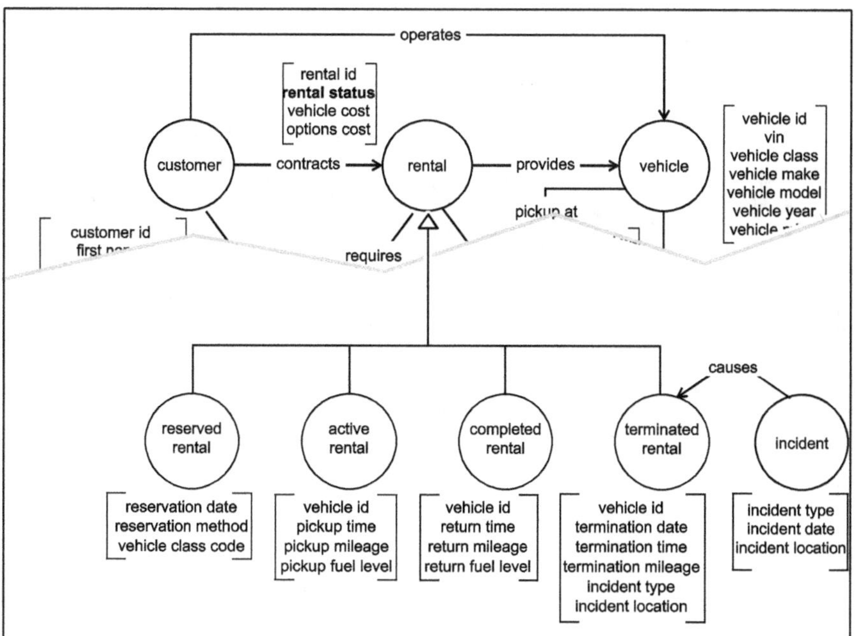

Figure 14: Rental Entity Taxonomy.

Relationship taxonomy classifies associations. Relationships can also have subtypes. Relationship subtypes add meaning when any of the subtypes have unique properties that are not true for all of the subtypes. In the vehicle rental domain, the customer-contracts-rental relationship has two subtypes: round-trip and one-way. A round-trip rental is the standard case in which a vehicle is picked up from and returned to the same location. With a one-way rental, the vehicle is picked up at one location and returned to another. For one-way rentals, additional information is needed: unique properties to record the one-way fee and the return location. Figure 15 illustrates this classification structure.

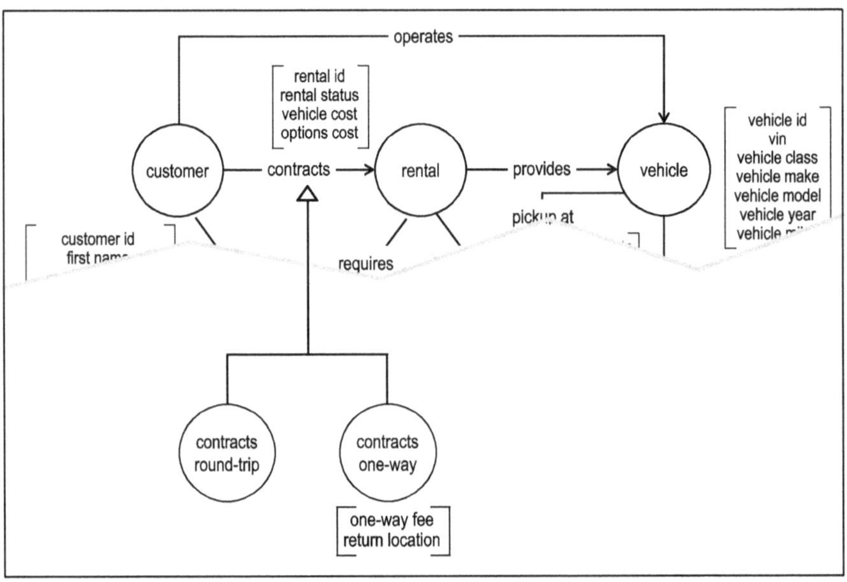

Figure 15: Relationship Taxonomy: Customer Contracts Rental.

Again, taxonomy analysis leads to terminology analysis. Each of the subtypes and both new properties need to be defined and described. The semantic distinction matters. Round-trip and one-way rentals have different economics, different logistics, and different analytical patterns. Distinguishing them in the semantic model and defining them clearly enables consumers to query and analyze them appropriately.

Property taxonomies classify values. Property taxonomies identify the defined classification structures for properties that contain categorical values. When a property describes categories but does not lead to an entity or relationship taxonomy, a property taxonomy can be used to describe the classification structure. In the vehicle rental model, payment type has three values: card payment, digital services payment, and EFT (electronic funds transfer). Payment status has three: requested, received, and declined. Location type has four: airport, hotel, suburban, and rural. Figure 16 shows how these are modeled as classification structures.

It is important to note that if any value classification structure requires additional properties (for example, a declined payment requiring a decline reason), then the entity or relationship taxonomy is the appropriate modeling technique. Properties taxonomy is used when the classification does not yield unique properties or relationships.

In the example on the following page, ten new terms have been added to the model, which means ten new definitions are needed. Property taxonomy makes controlled vocabulary explicit. Payment type, for example, is a defined set of values with documented meanings for each value. Property taxonomies directly support data integration and interoperability. If two systems track location type but they use different codes, the taxonomy provides the standard terms to which both can be mapped.

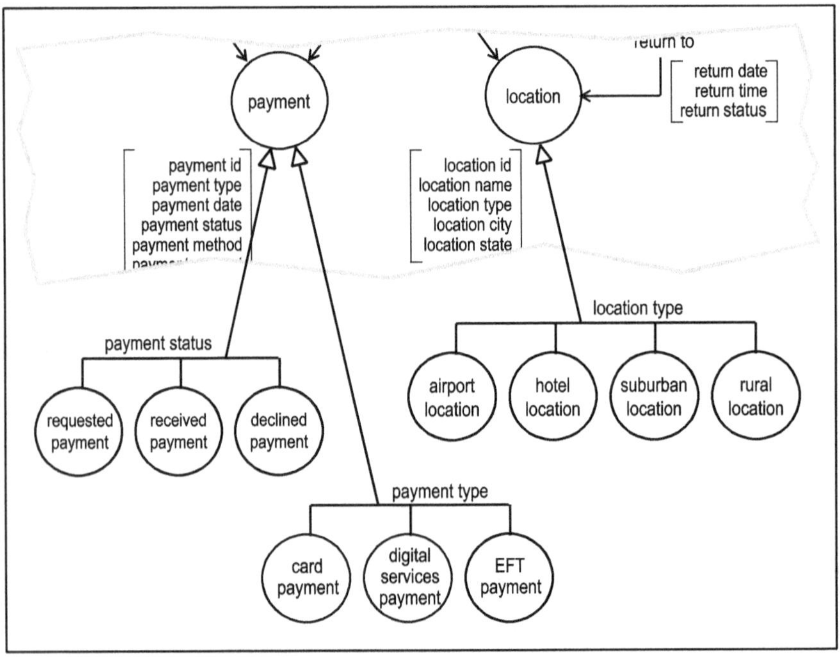

Figure 16: Property Taxonomies.

Putting it All Together

The complete semantic data model is the synthesis of all these analytical activities: ontology (concepts and relationships), taxonomy (classification structures for entities, relationships, and properties), properties (data attributes for all nodes and edges), and terminology (documented definitions and description of every term).

The diagram of the complete model is complex and detailed. As shown in Figure 17, it contains enough detail that it is difficult to read at the size that it is printed. That's okay for the purpose of this book. The intent is to illustrate the detail and complexity. And this is a relatively small model. Beginning with five core entities and eight relationships, it evolved through iterative analysis to include newly discovered entities of incident and legal action, four classification structures, sixteen subtypes, and more than fifty properties. Those are likely modest numbers when compared with your business domains. In practice, you'll want the diagram in digital form, with the ability to zoom in and out and navigate between detail and big-picture views.

Yes, it is complex. But every element of that complexity is the result of deliberate analysis with the intent to formally name and describe every term in the model. That's the work of semantics.

A few observations about the complete model are worth making.

First, the model is larger than the initial entity list suggested. The five original entities, through taxonomy analysis, expanded into a richer structure that includes rental lifecycle states, incident and legal action entities, and relationship subtypes. This expansion is normal and healthy. Semantic models earn their complexity through analysis.

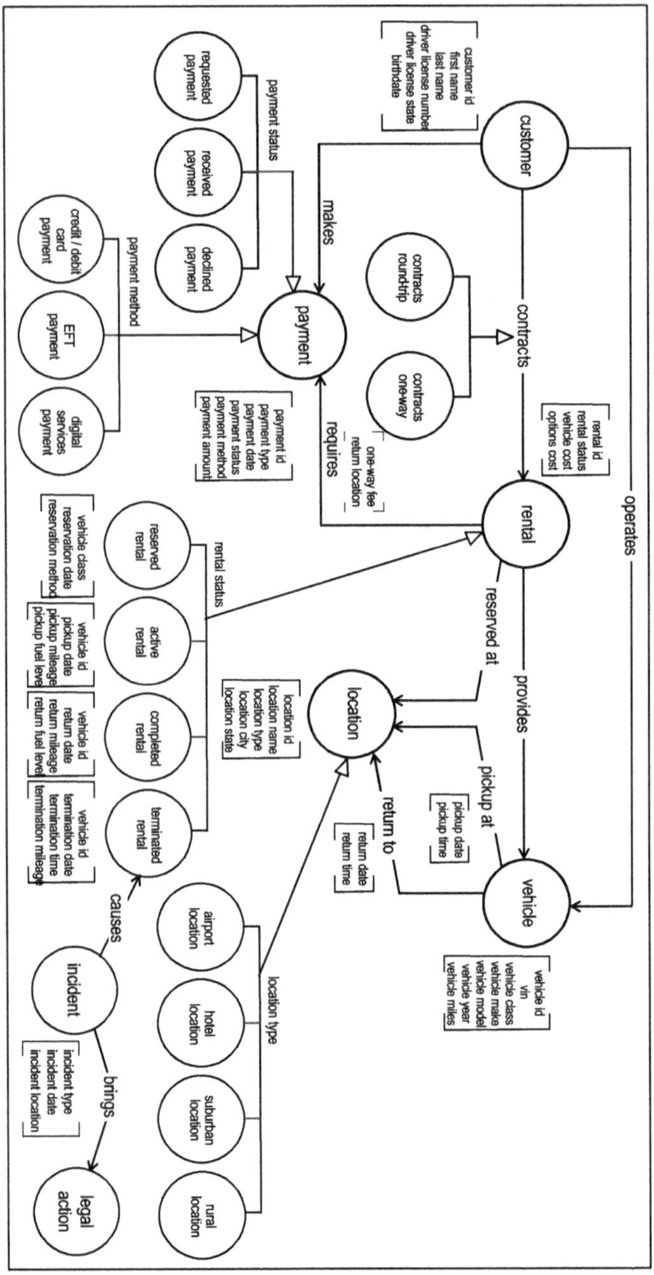

Figure 17: Vehicle Rental Domain Semantic Model.

Second, every term in the model has a definition. The diagram is the visual representation, but the definitions are equally important. A model without definitions is a diagram. A model with definitions is a semantic artifact.

Third, the model is a living document. It will be extended as new use cases surface new requirements, as business rules evolve, and as the organization's understanding of its own domain deepens. Design for evolution.

Semantic data modeling begins with the domain, not the data. The processes of entity analysis, relationship analysis, properties analysis, terminology analysis, and taxonomy analysis produce a complete ontology with corresponding taxonomies. A graph model accompanied by definitions and descriptions of every concept, relationship, and property expresses the full semantic meaning of a domain.

Graph models are well-suited to this work because they represent entities and relationships in a visual, intuitive form that is easily understood by business, data, and technology professionals. The vehicle rental model illustrates the range of modeling concepts: from the initial five-entity graph through taxonomy analysis, edge cases, and the surfacing of new entities through iterative refinement.

CHAPTER FOUR

Semantic Layers in Data Architecture

"Architecture is the thoughtful making of space."

Louis Kahn

The Semantic Model as Architectural Anchor

A semantic model is much more than passive documentation. It is the means to connect architecture components based on the meaning of data. In a well-designed data architecture, it is an active structural component that functions as the stable reference point to which all other components connect. Data sources map their schemas to the semantic model. Data consumers can query the semantic model without needing to understand or work directly with technical components or physical implementations. Integration and interoperability processes apply mappings defined in the semantic model to remediate data disparities and translate between local data dialects. Governance rules are often expressed in semantic terms.

This positioning creates a significant architectural benefit: the semantic model can remain stable even as the physical systems surrounding it change. When a source system modifies its schema, the mapping to the semantic model changes. The semantic model and the components and processes based upon it remain stable. That stability is the semantic model's most important architectural characteristic.

The semantic model is the stable center of a continuously changing data management world.

The five types of semantic layers introduced in Chapter 2 each play specific architectural roles. Understanding those roles is a key to purposeful architectural design. Architects choose which layers to build, where to place them, and how to sequence the work.

Semantic Layers in Architectural Context

Each semantic layer type occupies a distinct position in the data architecture and serves a specific architectural purpose. Figure 18 shows how they relate to the three primary architectural contexts: operations, pipelines, and analytics.

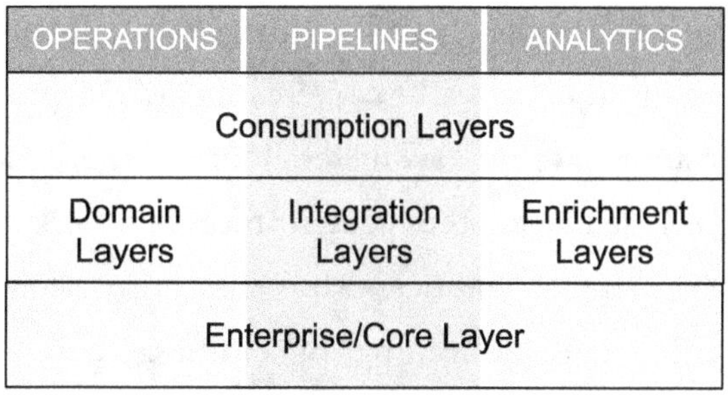

Figure 18: Semantic Layers in Architectural Context.

The enterprise or core layer spans all three contexts. It is the shared semantic foundation to which every other layer connects. Domain layers serve the operational context, expressing local meaning within business domains. Integration layers work within pipelines, reconciling meaning as data crosses domain and system boundaries. Enrichment layers serve the analytics context, capturing the meaning created as raw data is refined and aggregated. Consumption layers span all three contexts, providing meaning in the specific terms of whoever is consuming the data.

The Enterprise Layer as Architectural Foundation

The natural starting point for semantic architecture is the enterprise or core layer, which focuses on widely shared data: the concepts that every domain needs to agree on. Customer, product, account, employee: these are the entities that appear in nearly every business area and that create the most expensive reconciliation problems when they are not consistently defined.

The enterprise layer fits naturally with master data management. If your organization already operates an MDM program, you almost certainly have the raw material for an enterprise semantic layer. MDM manages the golden records: the authoritative instances of shared entities. The enterprise semantic layer manages the shared meaning of entities: their definitions, classifications, and relationships.

MDM governs identity: Who is Customer 12345?

Enterprise Semantics governs meaning:
What does "customer" mean and how is it related to everything else?

Together, MDM and an enterprise semantic layer form a powerful foundation. MDM ensures that every system agrees on who Customer 12345 is. The enterprise semantic layer ensures that every system agrees on what "customer" means, what properties a customer has, and how customers relate to other entities. Identity and meaning, both explicit and governed.

Domain Layers and Operational Data Management

Introducing domain semantic layers for operational systems requires architectural rethinking: moving from a model where each system manages its data independently to one in which systems are organized into domains, each with a governed semantic layer.

Domains group related systems around a set of closely related business capabilities. A Sales domain might include the CRM, sales force automation, and territory management systems. An Orders domain might include order entry, order management, and order fulfillment. A Financials domain might include accounts payable, accounts receivable, and the general ledger.

Each domain has a semantic layer that expresses the local meaning of data within that domain. The Sales domain semantic layer defines the meanings of "customer," "product," "opportunity," "quota," and "territory" in a sales context. The Orders domain defines what "order," "product," "line item," "fulfillment," and "return" mean. The term "product" appears in both, but the definitions differ: in Sales, a product is a catalog offering being positioned for a prospect; in Orders, it is a specific orderable item with a SKU, a unit price, and an inventory position. Both definitions are correct within their domain. The domain semantic layer makes that local meaning explicit. The enterprise semantic layer defines "product" at a level of abstraction that encompasses both: the thing the organization makes or sells, independent of how Sales positions it and how Orders tracks it.

Domain semantic layers serve two purposes simultaneously. Within the domain, they support consistency: every system in the Sales domain uses the same definitions for the same concepts.

Across domain boundaries, they provide a governed interface: other domains and the analytics infrastructure can access Sales domain data through the semantic layer without needing to understand the internal systems.

Domain Layers and Data Products

Domain semantic layers are a natural enabler of data products. A data product is a consumer-ready collection of accessible data designed to provide specific data functionality, but a data product is only as useful as its semantic clarity. Data consumers need to know what the data in a product means before they can use it correctly.

Domain semantic layers provide the semantic foundation for data products. A Sales data product is described by the Sales domain semantic layer. Its concepts, relationships, properties, and definitions are inherited from the domain layer. Consumers who understand the domain layer understand the product.

Data products also benefit from architectural clarity about data acquisition. A domain-organized architecture can support three acquisition patterns: batch (high latency, for large-volume historical loads), change data capture (low latency, for near-real-time synchronization), and streaming (real time, for event-driven data). The choice of acquisition pattern is both a semantic and a technical decision: it determines what "current" means for the data in the product.

Integration Layers: From ETL Coding to Semantic Mapping

Integration semantic layers address the reconciliation challenge: making data from different domains and systems interoperable without requiring every system to adopt a uniform schema.

The key shift that integration layers enable is this: data equivalence moves from ETL code to semantic mappings. Instead of writing transformation logic that embeds the knowledge that customer_id in the CRM system means the same thing as account_number in billing, you define a semantic mapping that expresses that equivalence explicitly. The mapping is documented, versioned, reusable, and governed.

When a source system changes, when the CRM adds a new field or renames an existing one, you update the semantic mapping, not every downstream ETL job. The semantic meaning remains stable; the physical plumbing is adjusted behind the scenes.

Data equivalence moves from ETL code to semantic mappings; from buried logic that can quietly fail to explicit and governed statements of meaning.

Integration layers also improve lineage. Tracing how a value in a data warehouse was derived from a value in a source system becomes a matter of following semantic mappings. The mappings are explicit statements of equivalence that are far easier to read than code.

The Enrichment Layer: Preserving Meaning Through Analytics Pipelines

The enrichment layer follows data through analytics pipelines, ensuring that meaning is preserved and made explicit as raw data becomes refined, curated, and aggregated.

As data moves through an analytical environment, from raw ingestion through successive refinement stages, it is transformed. Fields are computed. Records are joined. Aggregates are calculated. Each transformation creates derived data with new meaning. The enrichment layer explicitly captures that meaning.

When analysts work with curated data lacking an enrichment layer, they face the same semantic uncertainty as those working with raw data, except that curated data has less obvious lineage. A field that is descriptively named as thirty_day_rolling_avg_transaction_value is more likely to be interpreted correctly than cust_txn_val_raw, but its interpretation remains incomplete without knowing what counts as a transaction, how cancellations are handled, what period the rolling window covers, and what population the average is calculated over.

The enrichment layer captures those decisions explicitly, making derived data as semantically clear as source data.

Consumption Layers and Consumer Interfaces

Consumption layers provide the last-mile semantic interface: meaning applied in the specific context of a consumer's needs.

Different consumers need the same underlying data interpreted differently. A business intelligence dashboard for an executive team needs aggregated metrics in familiar business terms. A data science platform needs granular data with precise variable definitions and explicit statements of what transformations have been applied. An operational API needs real-time data with strong transactional semantics and predictable latency. An AI model needs data represented in terms that reflect the business concepts it needs to reason about.

A consumption layer contextualizes meaning.
It does not reinvent it.

Consumption layers are built on top of the more stable layers below. A consumption layer for an executive dashboard might define 'active customer' with a 90-day recency threshold. A consumption layer for a churn prediction model might use 30 days. Those definitions differ, but both reference the same underlying 'customer' concept from the enterprise layer. The variation is intentional and transparent, not a sign of inconsistency. Different consumers legitimately need different interpretations of the same data. The semantic foundation ensures those interpretations remain connected to a shared, governed definition.

This layering is what makes consumption-layer variation manageable. The shared semantic foundation is stable. The context-specific interpretations are transparent and documented.

From Implicit to Explicit Meaning

The five semantic layer types described in this chapter each address specific architectural challenges. Together they form a family of purposeful components that, when positioned appropriately, transform a data architecture from one where meaning is implicit and code-embedded to one where meaning is explicit, governed, and durable. The architectural purpose and positioning described in this chapter provide the framing needed before deciding how to implement semantic layers as working software.

CHAPTER FIVE

Implementing Semantic Data Layers

"In theory there is no difference between theory and practice. In practice there is."

Yogi Berra

From Architecture to Software

Architectural components describe what a semantic layer does. Implementation turns those components into working software. The gap between the two is where many semantic data initiatives stall. The concepts are sound, the architectural vision is compelling, but the path from concept to production is unclear.

This chapter addresses that gap. It describes five major implementation approaches: APIs, data products, data contracts, data virtualization, and schema registries. It also describes four implementation patterns that shape how semantic capabilities are realized in software. Together, these provide a decision framework for choosing among approaches and guidance on combining patterns to address multiple needs.

Implementation Approaches

Five implementation approaches are often used for semantic data layers. They are complementary, not mutually exclusive, and a mature semantic architecture typically employs several, each with a distinct role and its own trade-offs. They also blend naturally: a data product, for example, typically embeds both an API and a data contract.

Data contracts define the semantic agreement.
APIs enforce contracts at runtime.
Data products package APIs and contracts into units that consumers can discover, trust, and use.

Data Contracts are formal specifications that define structure, format, semantics, quality, and terms of use for data. A data contract functions as a service level agreement between a data provider and a data consumer, expressed in both machine-readable and human-readable form.

In a semantic architecture, data contracts formalize shared business meaning at system and product boundaries. A contract goes beyond the specification of the physical format (field names, data types, encoding) to include the semantic meaning of each field, the quality guarantees the provider makes, the privacy constraints that govern use, and the versioning policy that governs how changes will be communicated.

Data contracts make semantic agreements explicit and enforceable. A contract makes meaning at a system boundary explicit: written down, versioned, and subject to governance, expressed in documented form instead of embedded in developer memory or ETL code.

Data contracts are increasingly important for AI governance. If a model is trained on data from a specific source, the data contract describes what that data means and the assumptions the model makes. This is essential information for auditing, reproducing, and maintaining model behavior.

APIs operationalize data contracts. They are the runtime interface through which the terms of a contract are enforced. An Application Programming Interface is a software component that acts as a communication mechanism between applications. In a semantic architecture, APIs do more than expose data; they expose data through contracts that reflect shared business meaning.

A generic data API exposes a table: here are the columns, here are the rows, and here are the data types. A semantic API exposes a concept: here is a customer resource, with properties that correspond to the customer concept in the semantic model, subject to the rules and constraints expressed in that model. The consumer works in business terms. The API handles the translation to physical data structures. The API contract is itself a semantic artifact: it uses the vocabulary of the semantic model and enforces the constraints defined there.

APIs are particularly appropriate for the consumption layer and for integration between operational systems. The main governance challenge is drift: APIs that are developed independently, without reference to a shared semantic model, will develop their own local vocabularies and create a different kind of semantic inconsistency. API governance, ensuring that all APIs align with the enterprise semantic model, is the mitigation.

Data Products are consumer-ready collections of accessible data designed to provide clear, documented functionality. A data product is more than a dataset: it packages data, metadata, processing logic, and access interfaces (typically APIs that enforce the product's data contract) into a coherent unit that can be discovered, trusted, and used without needing to understand the underlying systems.

In a semantic architecture, data products carry semantic metadata: not just the physical format of data, but its business meaning. A well-designed data product is self-describing. A consumer who encounters it can understand what it contains, what the data means, how it was derived, what transformations have been applied, and what it can and cannot be used for.

Semantic layers make data products scale. Each data product inherits its definitions from the shared semantic model. Customer in Product A and Customer in Product B mean the same thing because both reference the same semantic definition. This consistency is the underlying principle of data product interoperability.

Data Virtualization provides access to data across multiple sources without physically moving or copying the data. Queries are executed at runtime, with the virtualization layer handling the translation between the semantic view the consumer sees and the physical schemas of the underlying sources.

A virtualization-based semantic layer operates in four tiers. At the lowest level, a connection layer provides physical connectivity to databases, files, APIs, and streams wherever they reside. Above that, a transformation layer handles consolidation: joining, filtering, and reshaping data from multiple sources. The semantic layer applies business meaning, translating physical schemas into semantic concepts defined in the semantic model. At the top, a consumption layer provides the consumer interface.

The advantages of virtualization are significant: no data duplication, real-time access, and the ability to change underlying sources without changing the consumer-facing semantic interface. The main challenges are performance (complex queries across many sources can be slow) and data quality (the virtualization layer works with the quality it receives from source systems).

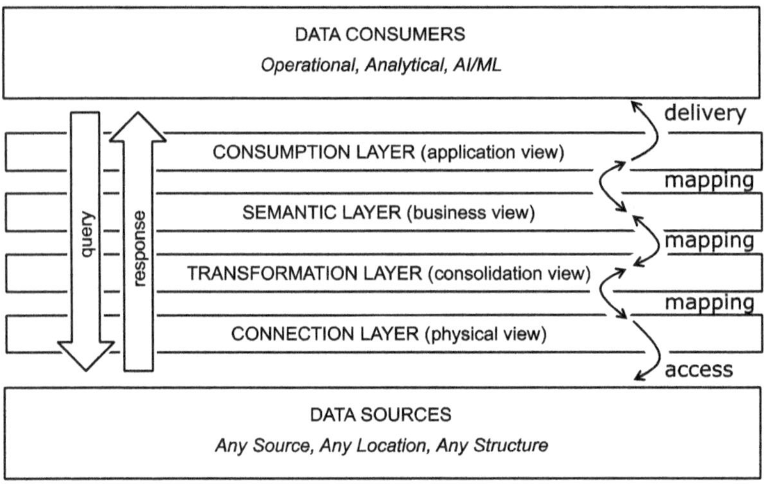

Figure 19: The Data Virtualization Stack.

Virtualization is well-suited to the integration layer and consumption layer. It is less suited to the enrichment layer, where persistent derived data is often necessary for performance at analytical scale.

Schema Registries are a practical approach to semantic layers for event-driven and streaming architectures. The four approaches above are primarily oriented toward request-response and batch patterns: a consumer requests data, and a governed interface delivers it. In event-driven and streaming architectures, the interaction works differently. Producers publish events to a stream; consumers subscribe and process them asynchronously.

Schema registries are the mechanism that enforces semantic governance in that context.

A schema registry is a centralized repository that stores and manages the schemas of messages exchanged across an event stream. When a producer publishes an event, the registry validates that the message conforms to a registered schema. When a consumer reads it, the registry provides the schema needed to interpret the message correctly. The schema defines both the structure (field names, data types) and the semantic meaning: what the customer_id field refers to, what currency an amount is expressed in, and what time_zone a timestamp uses.

Four Implementation Patterns

Beyond specific approaches, four implementation patterns describe the essential ways that semantic meaning can be realized in software. Each pattern has a distinct essence, specific characteristics, inherent strengths, and real limitations. Choosing among them, or combining them, requires understanding all four.

Metadata-Only: In the metadata-only pattern, semantics is represented as descriptive metadata that guides data access. Consumers interpret meaning at query time. Mediation is minimal; the pattern relies on user understanding and the capabilities of the tools that consumers use.

Metadata Only	Graph Based	Virtualization & Federation	APIs & Data Contracts
Semantics represented as descriptive metadata	Semantics materialized as entities and relationships	Semantic interpretation at query time across sources	Semantics enforced at system boundaries
Characteristics: Applied at query or access time; no data storage	**Characteristics:** Explicit modeling; durable semantic backbone	**Characteristics:** Distributed execution; minimal data movement	**Characteristics:** Schemas, APIs, and events as semantic contracts
Strengths: Fast time to value, strong usability	**Strengths:** Expressive, flexible, and well-aligned to semantic models	**Strengths:** Architectural flexibility; transitional architectures	**Strengths:** Clear ownership; strong boundary interoperability
Limitations: Narrow semantic scope; analytics-centric by design	**Limitations:** Requires modeling discipline and governance	**Limitations:** Performance sensitive; dependent on upstream semantics	**Limitations:** Risk of semantic drift without enterprise alignment

Figure 20: Semantic Layer Implementation Patterns.

Tableau's logical layer, Looker's LookML, Power BI's data model, and dbt's metrics layer are all metadata-only semantic layers. They apply business names, metric definitions, and field descriptions at query time without storing any additional data. The strengths are fast time to value and strong support for analytical usability.

The limitations are equally real. The metadata-only pattern is analytics-centric by design. It addresses the analytics layer; semantic challenges upstream (integration inconsistencies, identity mismatches, meaning lost in ETL pipelines, etc.) require deeper treatment. Semantic definitions expressed in a BI tool's metadata layer are typically tied to that tool's environment and not reusable outside it.

Metadata-only is a good starting point. It delivers immediate value for analytical use cases. But it should be recognized as a first step, not a complete solution.

Federation and Virtualization: In the federation and virtualization pattern, semantics is expressed as structural metadata used for mapping and binding, and meaning is resolved at query time through mediation and translation. Distributed execution across multiple sources minimizes data movement. This pattern provides architectural flexibility that other patterns cannot match. It works particularly well in transitional architectures, when moving from one architectural approach to another, because a virtualization layer can provide semantic access to existing sources without restructuring the physical architecture. Consumers see a stable semantic interface; the physical world can change behind the scenes.

The federation and virtualization pattern also excels for the integration layer, where real-time semantic reconciliation across multiple domains and sources is needed. Its limitations include performance sensitivity to complex queries and a reliance on the semantic quality of upstream sources.

Graph-Based: In the graph-based pattern, semantics is materialized as persistent graph structures. The semantic model, including ontology, taxonomy, properties, and definitions, is stored in a graph database. Meaning is resolved through the semantic model and graph navigation. The graph provides a durable semantic backbone that supports reuse and inference.

Inference is the distinctive capability that makes graph-based semantic layers uniquely powerful. A graph-based layer can reason about what it knows. If the model defines "sales representative" as a subclass of "employee," the layer can infer that all sales representatives are employees without an explicit mapping for that case. If a customer has made a purchase in a given region, and the model defines the relationship between purchases and regions, the layer can infer the customer's region affiliation. This inferencing enables greater flexibility than in other patterns.

The investment required for graph-based implementation is substantial: modeling discipline, graph technology expertise, and ongoing governance. For organizations with complex, multi-domain semantic requirements, particularly those building toward AI-ready architectures, that investment is well justified.

API-Based and Contract-Based: In the API-based and contract-based pattern, semantics is embedded in APIs, schemas, and data contracts. Meaning is enforced at interaction time through those interfaces. The pattern achieves strong encapsulation: each system owns its semantic interface and is responsible for maintaining it.

This pattern is the natural fit for data mesh architectures, where domain teams own their data products and the interfaces through which those products are accessed. Data contracts become the mechanism for expressing and enforcing the semantic interface of each product. Strong encapsulation produces clear ownership: the team that builds a product is responsible for its semantic integrity.

In event-driven and streaming architectures, schema registries are how this pattern is realized. The schema registry enforces the contract at the moment of event publication and consumption, serving the same role that an API contract serves in request-response architectures. The underlying pattern is the same: meaning is defined formally, owned by the producer, and enforced at the boundary.

The governance challenge is semantic drift. If domain teams develop APIs and contracts independently, without reference to a shared semantic model, individual interfaces can be internally consistent while collectively inconsistent across the enterprise. The mitigation is semantic governance: a shared semantic model that all contracts reference, combined with architectural review processes that catch divergence.

Which Patterns Fit Where?

Each implementation pattern serves some semantic layer types better than others. Understanding these affinities helps make implementation pattern choices purposeful and deliberate.

For domain and shared/core layers, graph-based and API/contract-based patterns are the strongest fits. These layers need to be expressive, persistent, and reusable: qualities that favor explicit, persistent semantic models.

For the integration layer, all three richer patterns (graph-based, federation/virtualization, and API/contract-based) provide strong support. Integration needs semantic reconciliation that operates across system boundaries, which all three can deliver.

Semantic Layer Types

	Domain	Enterprise	Integration	Enrichment	Consumption
Metadata-Only	weak	weak	weak	moderate	strong
Virtualization	moderate	moderate	strong	weak	moderate
Graph-Based	strong	strong	strong	moderate	moderate
APIs & Contracts	strong	strong	strong	weak	strong

Figure 21: Semantic Layer Types and Implementation Patterns.

For the enrichment layer, graph-based and API/contract-based patterns handle the explicit modeling of derived meaning most naturally. Metadata-only can support enrichment in simpler cases.

For the consumption layer, the metadata-only pattern is at its strongest. This is exactly the use case for which BI semantic layers were designed. Federation/virtualization and API/contract-based patterns also serve consumption well.

Choosing Patterns Based on Need

An equally useful framing is capability-based: "What do you most need your semantic layer to do?" Different needs point to different patterns.

Semantic Layer Needs

	Access & Usability	Cross System Integration	Sharing Across DOmains	Application Embedded Semantics	Exploration & Discovery
Metadata-Only	fast path to value	difficult	difficult	impractical	data catalog
Virtualization	limited	strong & adaptable	limited	impractical	limited
Graph-Based	strong & robust	strong & adaptable	strong & durable	complex	semantic search
APIs & Contracts	limited	limited	strong & durable	strong & adaptable	impractical

Figure 22: Semantic Layer Needs and Implementation Patterns.

Analytical usability (making data accessible and understandable to business and data analysts) is the strongest use case for metadata-only, which delivers a fast path to value. Graph-based is a richer alternative that works especially well for more complex environments.

Cross-system integration (combining data from disparate sources using consistent semantics) is where federation/virtualization and graph-based patterns both excel. API/contract-based works well for bounded integration between specific systems.

Establishing enterprise-wide semantic consistency across domains calls for graph-based or API/contract-based patterns: the two options with the depth and durability that shared meaning requires. Development teams building semantically consistent applications need semantics enforced at the application boundary. API/contract-based is the clear fit: contracts are precisely how that enforcement happens.

Data discovery (helping users find and understand data they do not know exists) is well served by metadata-only implementations as rich data catalogs, or by graph-based approaches with semantic search capabilities. Streaming and event-driven architectures have their own semantic governance requirements. API/contract-based is the right pattern here, with schema registries as the specific mechanism: the registry enforces the semantic contract at the moment of event publication, ensuring producers and consumers maintain a shared understanding of message meaning as schemas evolve. Most mature semantic architectures combine multiple patterns. Start with the pattern that addresses your most urgent need, design for extensibility, and add patterns as additional needs become priorities.

Semantic Layer Components in Operation

The six implementation components introduced in Chapter 2 (semantic model management, context and rule management, mapping and binding, mediation and translation, semantic services and processes, and access interface) are present in all four patterns, but they play different roles depending on which pattern is used. Understanding those roles clarifies what each pattern can and cannot do.

		METADATA ONLY	FEDERATED / VIRTUAL	GRAPH BASED	APIs & CONTRACTS
SEMANTIC MODEL MANAGEMENT	Store and manage semantic models	✓	✗	✓	✗
SEMANTIC MAPPING & BINDING	Connect physical data structures to meaning	✓	✓	✗	✓
SEMANTIC CONTEXT & RULE MANAGEMENT	Manage contextual interpretation	✗	✗	✓	✓
SEMANTIC MEDIATION & TRANSLATION	Apply mapping to reconcile disparity		✓	✗	
SEMANTIC ACCESS INTERFACE	Provide consumer-friendly access	✓	✓		✓
SEMANTIC SERVICES & PROCESSES	Execute semantic processing	✗		✓	✗

✓ Primary ✗ Supporting

Figure 23: Semantic Layer Components and Implementation Patterns.

In a **metadata-only** implementation, semantic model management, mapping and binding, and the access interface are the primary components. The metadata layer is the semantic model; mapping and binding connect field names and descriptions to semantic concepts; and the access interface is where consumers interact with the semantics directly. Context and rule management and semantic services play supporting roles: contextual rules and metric definitions can be expressed in metadata, and basic services support query-time interpretation. Mediation and translation are minimal: there is no runtime reconciliation across heterogeneous sources.

In a **federation and virtualization** implementation, mapping and binding, mediation and translation, and the access interface are the primary components. The mappings from physical schemas to semantic concepts are the core mechanism; runtime reconciliation across heterogeneous sources is what the pattern does; and the access interface delivers the unified semantic view to consumers. Semantic model management and context and rule management are supporting: both provide the definitions and rules that mappings and translations rely on. Semantic services and processes are minimal: the pattern's work is done through mapping and translation instead of processing.

In a **graph-based** implementation, semantic model management, context and rule management, and semantic services and processes are all primary. The graph is the semantic model. It stores the ontological rules, constraints, and contextual interpretations that enable inference. Inference, reasoning, and graph query capabilities are the pattern's distinctive value. Mapping, binding, mediation, and translation are supporting: they connect physical data to graph entities and enable reconciliation. Consumers interact through semantic services, with no need for a dedicated access layer.

In an **API/contract-based** implementation, the access interface, mapping and binding, and context and rule management are all primary. The APIs and contracts are the semantic layer itself; mapping and binding is primary because contracts encode mappings between internal data structures and semantic concepts; and context and rule management is primary because contracts are fundamentally documents of rules, constraints, and contextual definitions. Semantic model management, semantic services, and processes support a shared model to align contracts, and validation services enforce contract compliance. Mediation and translation are minimal: enforcement occurs at runtime through the contract, not through runtime reconciliation.

Semantic Layer Engineering

The work described in this chapter sits at a distinctive intersection. A semantic layer engineer needs the technical fluency of a data architect (physical data structures, integration patterns, implementation technologies), the software engineering discipline to work with formal, machine-readable artifacts (data contracts in YAML, graphs in RDF, schemas in Avro or Protobuf), the conceptual precision of a modeler (defining entities, relationships, and properties with rigor), and the organizational sensibility of a business analyst (understanding how different parts of the organization use and think about data). Most data roles require two or three of these. Work on the semantic layer requires all of them.

The technical dimension is real, but semantic layer engineering requires much more than technical perspectives. Choosing between a graph-based and an API/contract-based pattern, deciding when federation serves better than materialization: these require sound technical judgment. But the harder work is typically organizational. Getting domain experts to agree on a single definition of "customer," getting development teams to treat data contracts as first-class artifacts, persuading an organization to invest in shared meaning before the pain of inconsistency forces the issue: these are the challenges that determine whether semantic layer initiatives succeed or stall.

Semantic models, when well designed and well governed, are unusually durable. A physical data schema may be replaced when a system is modernized. A semantic model that accurately captures the structure of a business domain outlasts the systems that instantiate it. The engineer who builds a semantic model for a core business domain is building infrastructure the organization will rely on for years, possibly decades. That is a different kind of responsibility than building a pipeline or a dashboard, and it calls for a different kind of care.

The professional practice of semantic layer engineering is still forming. The technical foundations are solid and the business need is growing, but the career paths, communities of practice, and accumulated craft knowledge are still being established. The practitioners building this capability now are shaping what the discipline becomes. That is an unusual and genuinely interesting moment to be doing this work.

Chapter Six

Planning and Evolving Semantic Architecture

"The art of progress is to preserve order amid change and to preserve change amid order."

Alfred North Whitehead

Architects who think about semantic layers are managing a fundamental tension: the pressure to deliver value quickly and the importance of building something that evolves and matures over time. The decisions that matter most, including which layers to introduce, where to start, and how broadly to extend coverage, all reflect that tension.

Four architectural patterns describe where organizations are and where they are headed: from loosely connected systems with implicit meaning, through cohesive and semantics-based architectures, to AI-ready infrastructure where semantic layers ground both analytical and AI workloads. The patterns are useful for orientation but not prescriptive. The sequence in which semantic layers are introduced should be driven by where they create the most immediate value. That said, the patterns do carry rough dependencies. A semantics-based architecture builds on the domain structure and governed interfaces that a cohesive architecture establishes. An AI-ready architecture depends on the semantic foundation that precedes it. Organizations that reach for AI-ready infrastructure without that foundation tend to find that their AI systems are capable but unreliable, producing outputs that appear plausible on the surface but are not grounded in governed meaning.

Four Architectural Patterns

Loosely Connected Architecture

Most organizations start here, and this is, in fact, the current state for many today: operational systems as silos, connected by point-to-point data feeds, with a separate analytics infrastructure connected via ETL. Meaning is implicit and code-embedded. Two loosely coupled architectural worlds, operational and analytical, coexist without a shared semantic foundation.

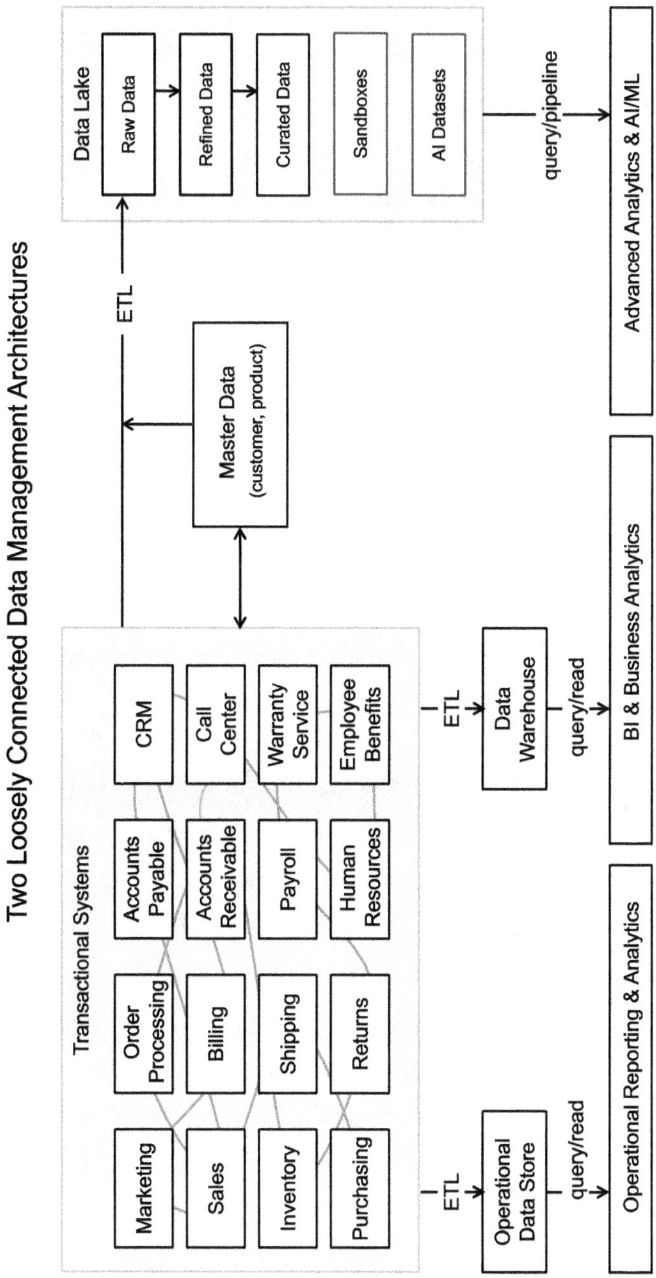

Figure 24: Loosely Connected Data Management Architectures.

Cohesive Architecture

A cohesive architecture reorganizes operational systems into domains, connects them to a unified analytics infrastructure through structured data acquisition pipelines, and introduces data products as governed interfaces between domains and consumers. The two architectural worlds become one.

The big shift here is the introduction of domain data management and data products. These are principles of data mesh architecture, but they can be adopted without a full data mesh commitment and without the organizational transformation that data mesh typically requires. And they provide a solid structure to introduce purposeful semantic data layers. Domains are a natural home for domain semantic layers, and data products benefit from both domain and consumption layers.

This shift is often as much organizational and governance work as it is technical. Defining domains, assigning ownership, and establishing governed interfaces requires commitment from business and technology leadership. A cohesive architecture creates the structural conditions that make broad-scale adoption of the semantic layer practical. It is a productive waypoint on the path to full interoperability, but semantic work can begin in a loosely connected architecture and deliver significant value before a full cohesive architecture is in place.

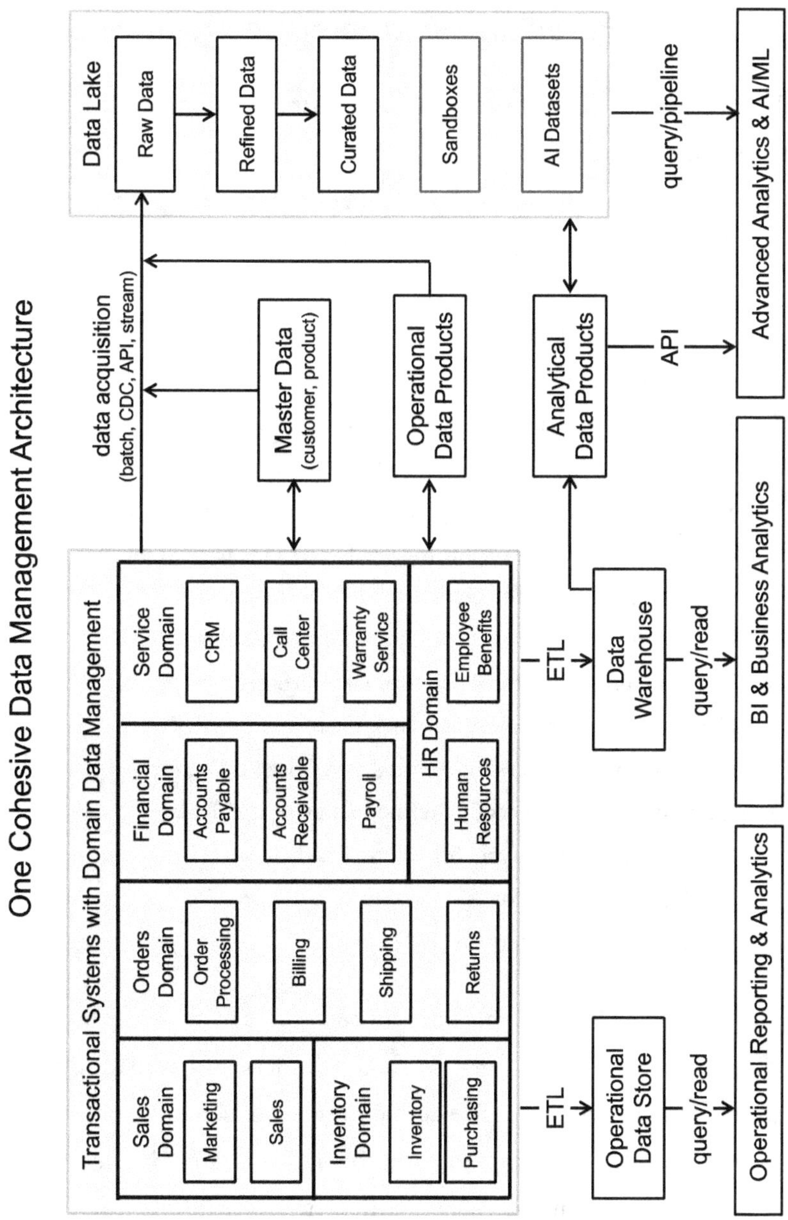

Figure 25: Cohesive Data Management Architecture.

Semantics-Based and Interoperable Architecture

The semantics-based architecture adds purposeful semantic layers throughout. The subtitle in Figure 26, "opportunities for many purposeful semantic layers," is deliberate. Sixteen opportunities are identified across the full architecture.

1. Domain Layers for each of six business domains
2. Integration Layer for the Operational Data Store
3. Consumption Layer for the Operational Data Store
4. Integration Layer for the Data Warehouse
5. Consumption Layer for the Data Warehouse
6. Enterprise Layer for Master Data Management
7. Consumption Layer for Master Data Management
8. Domain Layers for Operational Data Products
9. Consumption Layers for Operational Data Products
10. Domain Layers for Analytical Data Products
11. Consumption Layers for Analytical Data Products
12. Integration Layers for Refined and Curated Data
13. Enrichment Layers for Refined and Curated Data
14. Consumption Layers for Refined and Curated Data
15. Domain Layers for AI Datasets
16. Enrichment Layers for AI Datasets

The opportunities listed here are for categories of semantic layers, for example, domain layers for data products and consumption layers for data products. The actual number of semantic layers in a mature data environment will be considerably higher. An organization with many data products across multiple domains, and each serving distinct consumer groups, may have dozens of domain and consumption layers alone.

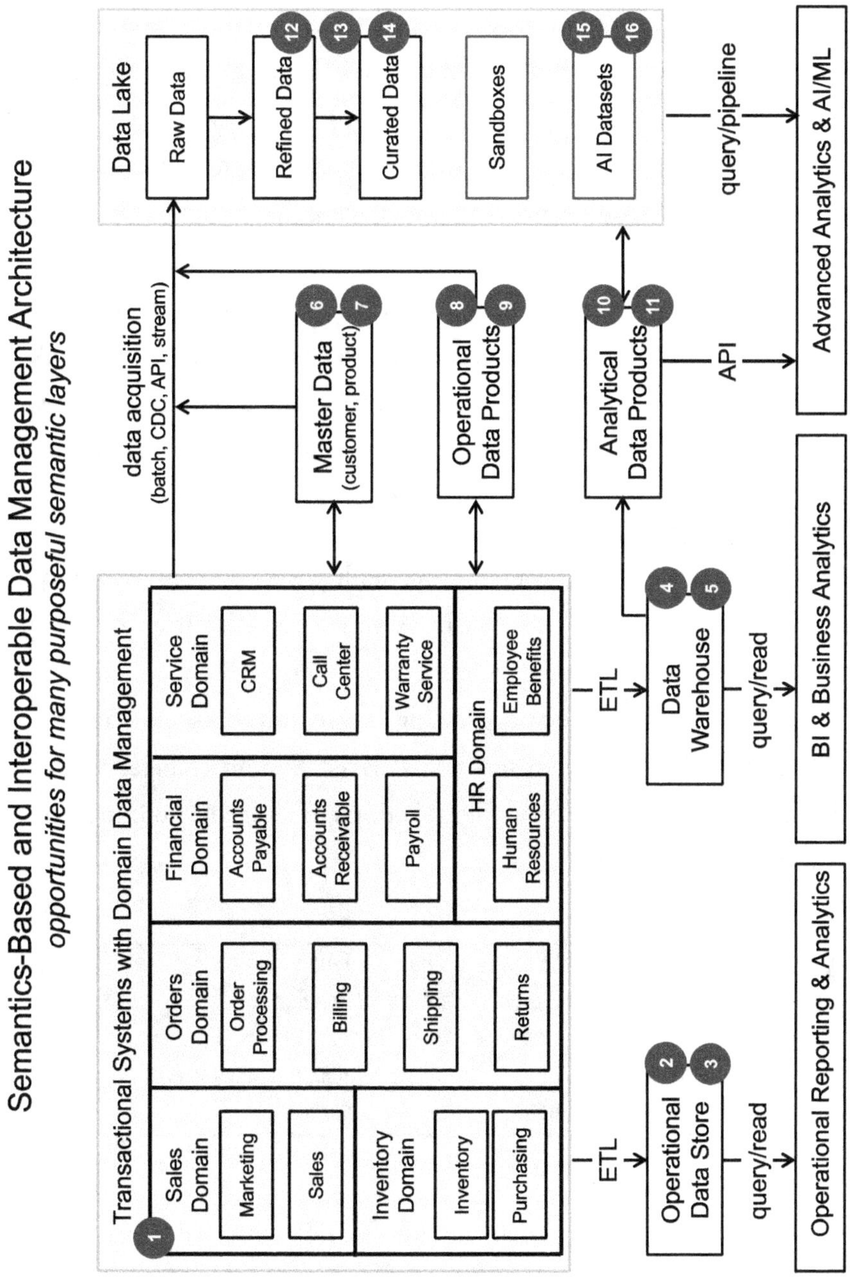

Figure 26: Semantics-Based Data Management Architecture.

This specificity matters. A semantics-based architecture is not a single semantic layer placed at one point in the architecture. It is a deliberate network of semantic layers, each serving a specific purpose at a specific architectural boundary. Some stabilize shared meaning across domains. Some govern the interface between operational systems and analytical infrastructure. Some document the meaning of curated data in the lake. Some govern the meaning of AI training data. The semantic layer is not one thing. Think "semantic layers," not "semantic layer." You need multiple layers, each with a purpose and placed where shared meaning creates real value.

In this architecture, data interoperability is a designed capability, not an accident. A new consumer can access data from multiple domains using shared semantic vocabulary. A new domain can join the architecture by expressing its semantics through a domain layer and mapping to the shared layer. System changes in one domain are contained within that domain and have no impact on consumers in other domains.

Semantic layers, domain data management,
and data products are complementary ideas.
Each amplifies the value of the others.
Together they make data interoperable, trustworthy, and
reusable across the enterprise.

AI-Ready Architecture

The AI-Ready architecture extends the semantics-based architecture to explicitly support artificial intelligence workloads. It adds components to support AI Assets and Resources. AI data assets include Training Data, Feature Store, Vector Database, and AI Datasets. Additional AI resources include a Prompt Store, and a Model Store and Registry. The data assets fit neatly as components of the data lake. The remaining resources reside outside the data lake, in the form of metadata and software. The table below briefly describes these additions.

AI Training Data	A large-scale repository for data used in training, tuning, and evaluation. Stores diverse structured, unstructured, and multimodal AI data.
Feature Store	A managed repository for reusable features used by AI and ML models. Supports consistency, reuse, and alignment between training and inference.
Vector Database	A database designed to store embeddings and support similarity search. Enables retrieval of contextually relevant content for AI applications.
AI Datasets	A managed repository for curated datasets prepared for AI use. Supports governance, repeatability, traceability, and dataset reuse.
Prompt Store	A managed repository for prompts, templates, and instructions. Supports reuse, consistency, improvement, governance, and version control.
Model Store & Registry	A managed repository and catalog for models and model metadata. Supports versioning, status tracking, governance, deployment, and reuse.

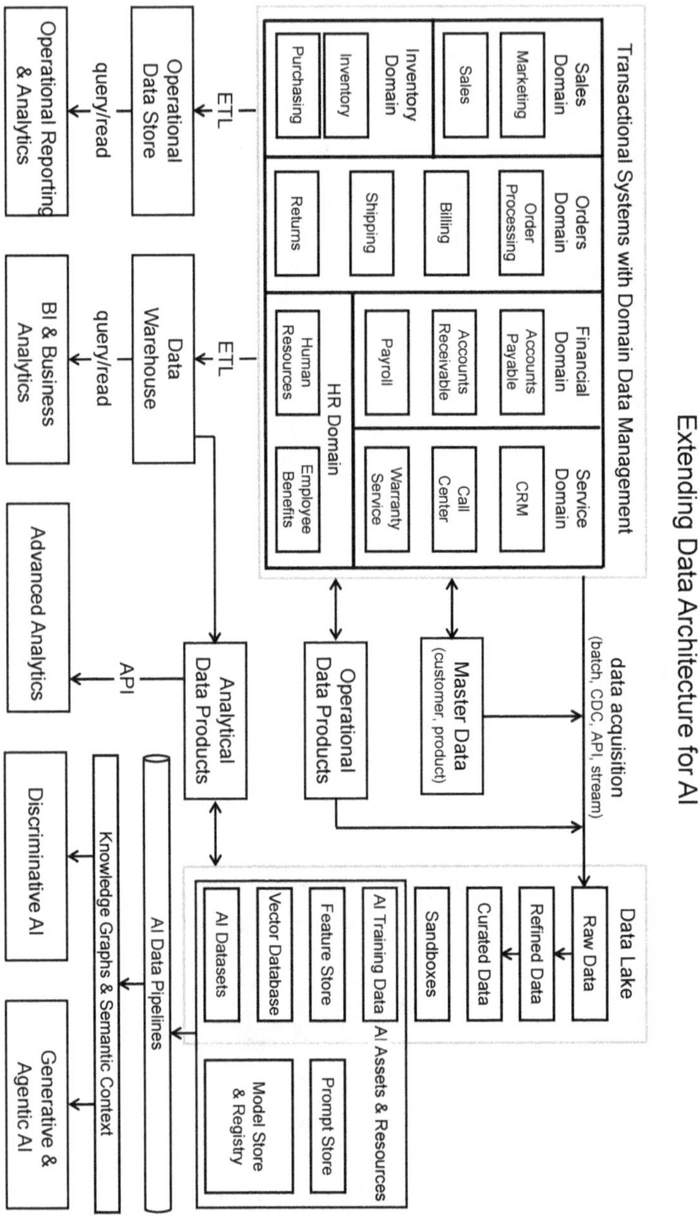

Figure 27: AI-Ready Data Management Architecture.

In addition to data assets and resources, knowledge graphs and semantic context are needed to support AI reliability. An enterprise layer provides organizational context. Domain layers provide context specific to the domains in which AI models operate. Enrichment layers add meaning when feature engineering derives or transforms data.

Semantic infrastructure built specifically for AI, without the governed shared meaning that earlier architectural patterns provide, produces AI systems that appear fluent but unreliable. The foundation comes first.

The AI-ready architecture is the most demanding of the four patterns. It requires the full semantic infrastructure of the semantics-based architecture as its foundation, then extends that foundation into AI-specific territory. Organizations that have invested in semantic layers in earlier architectural stages are well positioned for this extension. The semantic models, governed vocabulary, and data contracts that make data trustworthy for analysts are the same foundations that make data trustworthy for AI.

Where to Start

The right starting point is rarely the one that addresses everything. It is the one that delivers the most value relative to effort and creates the most useful foundation for what comes next.

For most organizations, that starting point is the enterprise or core layer, applied to the concepts most widely shared and most persistently problematic. Customer, product, and account are almost always on that list. Inconsistent customer definitions cause pain across sales, finance, service, and analytics. A core semantic layer that stabilizes those definitions delivers measurable value even without a broader architectural transformation underway. It also builds naturally on an existing MDM program: MDM provides the golden records; the enterprise semantic layer provides the shared meaning that makes those records interpretable across the organization.

A second practical starting point is an integration layer between two systems with high integration friction. If the connection between CRM and billing requires constant manual reconciliation, a semantic mapping that makes the equivalences explicit is a targeted investment with an immediate payoff. It requires understanding what the data means in each system and documenting the relationship between those meanings, but it does not require a domain reorganization or a new data platform.

Beyond these two common entry points, a few architectural questions can help identify the right starting place for a specific organization:

- **Where is semantic inconsistency causing the most visible pain?** The highest-friction point is usually a good starting point, because the value of addressing it is immediately demonstrable. When the cost of inconsistent meaning is diffuse and invisible, semantic investment is hard to justify. When it is concentrated and visible (in a report no one trusts, in an integration that requires constant manual correction, in an AI output that confidently produces wrong answers), the case is easy to make and the win is easy to show.

- **Where does data cross the most boundaries?** Semantic inconsistency multiplies at boundaries. A concept that is interpreted differently by three systems creates three times the reconciliation work of a concept interpreted differently by one. High-traffic boundaries, where data flows between many systems or serves many consumers, are a place where a semantic layer has strong architectural leverage.

- **Where does existing investment already create a foundation?** An MDM program, a governed data warehouse, a mature data catalog, or a well-managed domain is a partial semantic foundation. Starting where that investment exists means building on what already exists without starting from scratch. It also tends to accelerate delivery because the domain knowledge and stakeholder relationships needed for semantic work are already in place.

- **Where is the semantic model most stable?** Customer, product, and order change slowly. Starting with stable concepts means less rework as the architecture grows, and it reduces the risk that the initial investment becomes obsolete before it has been fully exploited.

Starting choices are not permanent commitments. The value of a good starting point is as much organizational as architectural: a visible win builds credibility, demonstrates that semantic investment pays off, and creates the momentum needed to justify the next investment. Start where the work will succeed, the value will be visible, and the foundation will support what comes next.

How Much Coverage Is Needed?

Not every operational system needs to be organized as a domain, and not every domain needs the same depth of semantic treatment. The systems that benefit most from semantic layers share certain characteristics: they are data sources for multiple consumers, they participate in multiple integrations, their data is used in analytical or AI contexts where meaning matters, or they operate under regulatory requirements where precise definitions carry compliance implications. Systems that are narrowly operational and share data with few others may need little semantic treatment.

The question is not how to cover everything.
It is where shared meaning creates the most value and where its absence incurs the greatest cost.

Domain organization follows the same logic. A Sales domain that touches customers, products, orders, and revenue reporting is an obvious candidate. A standalone employee benefits system that serves HR and payroll may not be. The questions architects should ask are where shared meaning creates the greatest value, and where the absence of shared meaning creates the greatest cost. Coverage should follow that analysis, not the organizational chart.

Sequencing the Work

The path toward a semantics-based and interoperable architecture is built incrementally, with each addition expanding what the organization can do with its data. AI-ready architecture is the natural next horizon, and the semantic foundation built in earlier stages is what makes it achievable.

A practical sequence often looks like this: start with an enterprise layer for the most widely shared concepts; extend to domain layers for the highest-value operational domains; build integration layers at the boundaries where integration friction is highest; add enrichment and consumption layers as the analytical and AI infrastructure matures. Organizations with active AI programs will begin to see the AI-ready pattern emerging naturally from that progression: the knowledge graphs, feature stores, and AI dataset governance that pattern requires all build on semantic infrastructure already in place.

But this is guidance, not a rule. An organization with a mature data warehouse and a growing AI program might find that consumption layers are the highest-value next step. An organization with severe cross-system integration problems might prioritize integration layers from the start. The architecture serves the organization's needs, and the sequencing should reflect that.

Sequencing should always start with the most stable. Customer, product, and order change slowly. Semantic layers built on stable concepts require less rework as the architecture grows. Layers built on volatile concepts become a maintenance burden.

The Parallel Path: Semantic Modeling and Architectural Evolution

Architectural evolution and semantic model evolution are not separate tracks. They run in parallel, and each enables the other. Introducing a domain semantic layer requires a domain semantic model. That model must be built before the layer can be implemented. As the architecture grows, the models grow with it. When a new domain joins the architecture, its domain model must be developed and its concepts mapped to the enterprise layer. When an integration layer is introduced at a domain boundary, the semantic mappings that layer relies on are a modeling artifact. When an enrichment layer captures the meaning of a derived metric, it is extending the semantic model into the analytics pipeline.

Semantic architecture and semantic modeling evolve in parallel. Each architectural stage requires a corresponding modeling stage. Planning for one means planning for both.

The iterative nature of semantic modeling described in Chapter 3 is not just a modeling technique. It is the rhythm of architectural evolution. Each architectural stage requires a corresponding modeling stage. The enterprise layer needs a core ontology. Domain layers need domain-specific models with local vocabulary and taxonomy. Integration layers need cross-domain mappings. Enrichment layers need documented derivation logic. Consumption layers need context-specific interpretations.

Planning for architectural evolution means planning for the modeling work that makes each stage possible. Organizations that treat semantic modeling as a front-loaded exercise and architectural implementation as a separate subsequent phase often find that their models are disconnected from the architecture they are meant to serve. The two should grow together.

Designing for Evolution

Semantic architectures designed to evolve outlast those designed to be complete. A few principles help:

- **Start with the most stable concepts**: Customer, product, order: these change slowly. Building semantic layers on stable foundations means less rework as the architecture grows. Layers built on stable concepts become the reliable reference points that the rest of the architecture depends on.

- **Design for extension**: Domain layers should be designed with the expectation that new systems will join the domain. Integration layers should anticipate new mappings as the source landscape changes. The semantic model is always in progress, and the architecture should accommodate that without requiring structural rework each time something new is added.

- **Govern the semantic layer explicitly**: The semantic model is a shared organizational asset. It needs ownership, versioning, change management, and a clear process for resolving definitional disputes. Semantic governance is not bureaucratic overhead. It is what keeps the model accurate and useful as the organization and its data environment change. A well-governed semantic model becomes more valuable over time. One that is left ungoverned drifts into inconsistency and loses the trust of the people who depend on it.

Principles for Your Architectural Journey

For you, as an architect with a stake in how your organization's data infrastructure evolves, the patterns in this chapter describe the terrain but not the path. The path depends on where your organization is starting, what is creating the most friction, where the most value is waiting to be unlocked, and what your stakeholders are ready to support. Good architectural judgment is understanding the forces that make some sequences work better than others, and making deliberate choices in light of those forces. These principles are a guide to that kind of thinking.

Follow the value, not the org chart. Coverage decisions driven by organizational structure tend to produce semantic layers that reflect political boundaries instead of data flows. The more productive question is always where shared meaning creates the most value and where its absence creates the most cost. Start there.

Stable concepts before volatile ones. The semantic model is only as durable as the concepts on which it is built. Customer, product, and order change slowly. Semantic layers built on volatile concepts become a maintenance burden before they become an asset.

The model and the architecture grow together. Semantic modeling and architectural evolution are not sequential activities: modeling comes first, followed by architecture. Each architectural stage requires a corresponding modeling stage. Planning for one without planning for the other is how organizations end up with architectures that outpace their models, or models that are disconnected from the architecture they were meant to serve.

The foundation comes before the frontier. AI-ready architecture is built on semantics-based architecture. The sequence is not bureaucratic caution; it is the dependency structure of the architecture itself. Organizations that establish the semantic foundation first find that AI-ready infrastructure follows naturally. Those that skip to the frontier find that the infrastructure is capable but not trustworthy.

Design for where you are going, not just where you are. Each architectural decision either opens or closes future options. Domain layers designed for a single system are harder to extend than those designed for a domain. Integration layers designed for two systems are harder to generalize than those designed for a pattern. The investment in forward-looking design pays for itself in reduced rework.

Architecture is a direction, not a destination. The four patterns in this chapter describe a journey, not a checklist. Few organizations will move cleanly from one to the next. Most will work in multiple patterns simultaneously, advancing in some areas while consolidating in others. What matters is not where you are in the sequence but whether each investment is building toward something more capable, more consistent, and more durable than what came before.

Chapter Seven

Putting It into Practice

"The secret of getting ahead is getting started."

Mark Twain

The concepts in this book (semantic data layers, ontologies, taxonomies, architectural patterns, implementation approaches) are only valuable if they lead to action. This chapter is about action: how to take what you have learned and apply it in your own organization.

Applying the Principles

Five principles frame a practical approach.

Start with a Clearly Defined Semantic Model for a Focused Domain

Start with one domain, the one with the most pressing semantic challenges, the most motivated stakeholders, or the most impactful downstream use cases. Build a complete, high-quality semantic model for that domain. Define every term. Deliver value. Then expand.

The risk is scope creep disguised as ambition. An enterprise-wide semantic architecture sounds more impressive than a focused domain model, but an ambitious model never finished delivers no value. A focused model that works, that people use, and that demonstrably reduces data friction is worth far more, and it creates the credibility and organizational buy-in needed to justify expanding the effort.

Identify Where Semantic Inconsistency Causes Friction Today

The best place to start is where semantic problems are currently creating real costs:

- Where are analysts spending time reconciling conflicting numbers?
- Where does data integration require the most manual intervention?
- Where do different teams routinely interpret the same data differently?

- Where do new team members struggle to understand what the data means?

Semantics addresses real problems. Finding the real problems first, before turning to architectural vision, ensures that the investment pays off quickly and visibly.

Introduce Semantic Layers Where Meaning Needs to Be Stabilized or Shared

Semantic layers have implementation costs. They should be introduced where the payoff is highest: where inconsistent meaning is causing the most pain, where data crosses the most boundaries, where the most consumers need access to the same concepts.

Not every part of your architecture needs a semantic layer. Local systems that serve a single team with no integration requirements may not justify the investment. Focus semantic effort where it creates shared value.

Select Implementation Patterns Based on Specific Needs

Choose an implementation pattern based on what you need to achieve, not because it is technically interesting or vendor-promoted. If your primary need is analytical usability, metadata-only gets you there quickly. If your primary need is cross-domain integration, graph-based or federation/virtualization is more appropriate. Let needs drive choices.

Evolve Incrementally: Semantics Grows With Use

The best semantic models are built over time, as users discover ambiguities, new use cases surface new requirements, and the organization's understanding of its domain deepens. Design for evolution from the start. Expect the model to grow. Welcome the revisions that come from real use: they mean the model is being used.

Assessing the Current State

Before deciding where to invest in semantic data layers, it is worthwhile to objectively assess your current state. The questions below are diagnostic tools, not rhetorical ones. The answers will tell you where semantic investment is most needed and most likely to deliver rapid value.

CURRENT STATE ASSESSMENT	
Meaning	Where does inconsistent meaning create confusion or rework today? How often do people interpret the same data differently? How much do people rely on local knowledge to understand data Are definitions documented and used consistently?
Domain Semantics	Do your key business domains have clearly defined concepts? Are terms and definitions consistent within a domain?
Integration & Interoperability	Where do systems struggle to exchange or align data? How much effort is spent reconciling data across systems? Are integration problems mostly technical, or do they arise from differences in meaning? Do shared concepts like customer & product mean the same thing across business areas?
Architecture	Where would separating meaning from data structures reduce complexity? Do different use cases (operational, analytical, AI) interpret the same data differently?
Implementation & Delivery	Do your APIs and data products clearly explain data meaning? When data is shared, is the meaning clear to those who receive it?

Figure 28: Current State Assessment Questions.

- **Where does inconsistent meaning create confusion or rework today?** This is the most direct question, and often the hardest to answer because the costs of semantic inconsistency are diffuse. They show up as time spent in meetings arguing over numbers, as manual reconciliation work that no one has formally budgeted for, as decisions made on data that was being misinterpreted.

- **How often do people interpret the same data differently?** A simple test: ask five people in your organization to define "active customer." If you get five different answers, you have a semantics problem. If everyone agrees immediately and produces consistent definitions, you may already be in better shape than most.

- **How much do people rely on local knowledge to understand data?** If onboarding a new data analyst requires weeks of informal education, sitting with experienced colleagues to learn what fields mean, what codes represent, what exceptions apply, that tribal knowledge is both a risk and a target for semantic documentation.

- **Are definitions documented and used consistently?** Many organizations have a data dictionary. Far fewer have definitions that are current, precise, and actually referenced by the people who use the data. Existence of documentation is not the same as usability of documentation.

- **Do your key business domains have clearly defined concepts?** Could you write down a definition of "order" that everyone in the Orders domain would agree with? How long would the discussion take? The length of that discussion is a measure of your semantic debt.

- **Are terms and definitions consistent within a domain?** Intra-domain consistency is the prerequisite for inter-domain interoperability. If a domain cannot agree internally on what its concepts mean, it cannot reliably share those concepts with others.

- **Where do systems struggle to exchange or align data?** Most organizations can name these points immediately: they are the sources of the most expensive and most frequent integration problems.

- **How much effort is spent reconciling data across systems?** Quantifying this effort, even roughly, builds the business case for semantic investment. If data reconciliation consumes 20% of your analytics team's time, a semantic layer that reduces it by half pays for itself quickly.

- **Are integration problems mostly technical, or do they arise from differences in meaning?** This distinction is important. Technical integration problems (different protocols, formats, or network zones) are solved through engineering. Semantic integration problems (different definitions, different identifiers, different classification schemes) require semantic work first. Applying technical solutions to semantic problems produces brittle integrations that fail in unexpected ways.

- **Do shared concepts like customer and product mean the same thing across business areas?** The answer to this question predicts a great deal about the cost and complexity of your integration challenges.

- **Where would separating meaning from data structures reduce complexity?** Consider the places in your architecture where meaning is most deeply embedded in code: the ETL jobs that contain the most transformation logic, the API integrations that do the most semantic translation. Those are the places where a semantic layer would create the most architectural leverage.

- **Do different use cases, such as operational, analytical, and AI, interpret the same data differently?** If so, a consumption-layer semantic architecture that explicitly manages those contextual differences may be more appropriate than enforcing a single interpretation across all use cases.

- **Do your APIs and data products clearly explain data meaning?** Consumers who cannot understand a product's semantic content without asking the producer are experiencing semantic friction. Well-documented APIs and data products reduce that friction.

- **When data is shared, is the meaning clear to those who receive it?** A useful test: share a data extract with a colleague who was not involved in creating it, and ask them to explain what each field means. The gaps in their explanation are the semantic documentation gaps.

Best Practices for Data Semantics

These ten practices represent the accumulated wisdom of semantic data management work across many organizations and contexts. They are ongoing disciplines, not sequential steps.

1. **Define terms clearly and consistently:** Use shared definitions. Avoid assumed meaning. This is the most fundamental practice and the hardest to sustain. Writing precise definitions requires getting agreement, sometimes contentious agreement, across teams that have developed their own local vocabularies. But the investment pays for itself many times over in reduced confusion, faster onboarding, and more reliable data.

A useful standard for a good definition: it should be precise enough that two people, reading it independently, would agree on whether any given instance satisfies it. Vague definitions that leave room for multiple interpretations create a false sense of shared meaning, which can be worse than no definition at all.

2. **Start with business concepts:** Start with business concepts before looking at data structures. Model real-world things and relationships first. One of the most common mistakes in semantic modeling initiatives is jumping to database schemas and asking "how do we model this?" instead of starting with "what real-world things are we representing, and how do they relate?"

   Schemas represent a team's decisions about how to store data at a particular moment in time. They encode history as much as meaning. Starting with schemas means inheriting all of that historical baggage, including the confusions, compromises, and simplifications that made sense in context but that do not reflect the domain as it should be understood. Start with the domain.

3. **Separate meaning from implementation:** Keep semantic models independent of systems and schemas. This is the core architectural principle that makes semantic layers durable. Systems are replaced. Schemas change. Technologies evolve. Meaning, when it has been properly defined, is more stable than any of these.

A semantic model entangled with a specific technology or schema becomes brittle when that technology or schema changes. A semantic model expressed independently of any particular implementation can survive those changes, serving as the stable reference point through architectural transitions.

4. **Establish a controlled vocabulary:** Standardize names, definitions, and classifications. If there are two acceptable ways to refer to the same concept, there will be twenty ways in practice. Controlled vocabulary reduces that variation and creates the shared language that makes consistent data management possible.

   Controlled vocabulary does not mean eliminating local terminology. It means documenting local terminology, mapping it to standard terms, and ensuring that the standard terms are used in all shared interfaces and integrations. People can continue to use "renter" in conversation; the semantic model uses "customer" as the standard term, with a note that "renter" is a common synonym.

5. **Make context explicit:** "Customer" does not mean exactly the same thing in Sales, Billing, and Service. Treating it as though it does will create as many problems as it solves. The right response is to document the standard definition and the domain-specific

variations, and to make the relationships among them explicit in the semantic model.

6. **Use semantics to guide integration:** Align meaning before mapping data. Most data integration projects start with schemas and discover meaning problems after the physical work has been done. Starting with semantics, asking what each system's data represents and how it maps to a shared semantic model, prevents the late-stage surprises that cause integration projects to overrun.

7. **Apply semantics at boundaries:** Embed meaning in APIs, contracts, and data products. Every system boundary is an opportunity to make semantics explicit and enforceable. A data product that ships with documented semantic metadata is self-describing. An API that enforces semantic contracts reduces the surface area for misinterpretation. Boundaries are where semantic discipline has the highest leverage.

8. **Combine implementation patterns:** Use metadata, graphs, APIs, and virtualization where each fits best. Metadata-only is appropriate for analytics consumption layers; graph-based is appropriate for shared enterprise concepts; API/contract-based is appropriate for operational system boundaries; federation/virtualization is appropriate for transitional integration scenarios. A mature semantic architecture uses the right pattern for each context.

9. **Design for reuse and evolution:** Expect meaning to grow and change over time. New use cases will surface new concepts. Business rules will evolve. Organizational structures will change. A semantic model designed as a closed, complete specification will quickly become out of date. A semantic model designed to be extensible, one that makes it easy to add new concepts, new relationships, and new contextual interpretations, will remain useful for years.

10. **Keep It practical and incremental:** Start small, deliver value, and expand as you use it. The organizations that succeed with semantic data layers are those that identify a real problem, solve it well, demonstrate its value, and build from there. Designing perfect enterprise-wide architectures in isolation rarely succeeds.

Incremental delivery is not a compromise. It is the right strategy. Each increment delivers value, generates feedback, builds organizational capability, and creates the credibility that sustains continued investment.

The Broader Significance

Data semantics is not a new idea. Librarians have understood the importance of controlled vocabulary and classification schemes for centuries. Philosophers have studied ontology for millennia.

What is new is the scale of the challenge: the volume of data, the number of systems, the pace of change, and the criticality of data-driven decisions have all grown to the point where informal, person-dependent approaches to data meaning can no longer keep up.

Semantic data layers are the engineering response to that challenge: a systematic, architectural approach to making meaning explicit, consistent, portable, and durable. They are not a technology product. They are a discipline, practiced through careful modeling, governed through clear ownership, and sustained through organizational commitment.

The organizations that invest in that discipline will find that their data becomes a durable asset and a valuable resource: one where the meaning attached to the data is clear, shared, and trustworthy. In a world where most organizations are drowning in data but starving for understanding, that is a meaningful advantage.

Where to Begin

If you have read this far and are wondering where to start, here is the simplest possible answer: find the data that matters most to your organization and make sure everyone agrees on what it means.

Pick one concept, such as customer, product, order, or whatever is most central to your business, and work through the modeling process described in Chapter 3. Set the scope. Identify the entities. Map the relationships. Analyze the properties. Work through the taxonomy. Write the definitions. Do it with the people who know the domain. Get all of the right people involved.

That single exercise will reveal more about your organization's semantic challenges than any abstract assessment. It will surface the disagreements, local dialects, undocumented rules, and implicit assumptions currently embedded in code and organizational memory. And it will produce something tangible: a semantic model that can serve as the foundation for everything that follows.

From that foundation, the work grows naturally. A semantic model for one concept suggests the concepts it relates to. A working semantic layer for one domain creates the template for the next. A demonstrated capability for consistent meaning in one integration enables confidence for the next.

Semantics grows through use. Start using it.

Index

active customer, 1, 15, 16, 69, 113
agentic systems, 2
analytical environments, 27
analytics infrastructure, 13, 66, 90, 92
application programming interfaces (APIs), 2, 28, 33, 69, 72, 73, 74, 75, 80, 81, 82, 83, 84, 86, 87, 115, 116, 119
architecture, 2, 22, 23, 61, 66, 79, 90, 92, 94, 96, 97, 99, 101, 103, 104, 105, 106, 107, 108, 111, 115
artificial intelligence (AI)
  AI-ready architecture, 2, 80, 90, 99, 103, 108
  data preparation, 13, 27
  models, 28, 69, 99
  readiness, 2
business concepts, 23, 25, 34, 69, 117
business glossary, 1
business intelligence, 28, 69
business vocabulary, 11, 16
classification, 7, 11, 28, 30, 31, 33, 51, 54, 55, 56, 57, 64, 115, 118, 120
context, 2, 5, 23, 26, 27, 28, 29, 30, 31, 39, 45, 49, 63, 65, 69, 70, 77, 84, 86, 99, 105, 117, 118, 119
  analytical, 30
  context-sensitive meaning, 31
  operational, 30, 63
  organizational, 30, 31, 99
  regulatory, 30
  semantic, 30, 99
controlled vocabulary, 7, 45, 46, 55, 118, 120
curated data, 68, 96, 97
data access, 11, 27, 77, 83
  self-service, 12, 16
data architecture, 23, 61, 62, 70
data catalogs, 16, 84, 101
data chaos, 19
data consumers, 17, 23
data contracts, 2, 72, 73, 74, 80, 87, 88, 99
data dictionary, 1, 113
data disparity, 18
data engineering, 15
data friction, 19, 110
data integration, 11, 13, 56, 110, 119
data interoperability, 11, 26, 35, 56, 62, 75, 92, 96, 114
data lakes, 1, 13, 97
data lineage, 68
data management, 1, 2, 3, 6, 10, 13, 21, 23, 26, 62, 92, 96, 116, 118
data meaning, 12, 13, 21, 116, 121
data models, 18, 59, 78
data objects, 9
data platforms, 100
data products, 2, 66, 72, 74, 75, 80, 92, 94, 96, 116, 119
data quality, 76
data reuse, 12
data semantics, 9, 18
data sources, 18, 23, 102
data sprawl, 18
data structure, 13, 21, 86, 115, 117

data supply chain, 34
data transformation, 13, 26
data virtualization, 2, 72, 75, 79, 82, 83, 111, 119
data warehouses, 13, 68, 101, 104
database management systems (DBMS), 6
definitions
  shared, 116
derived data, 68, 69, 76
derived metrics, 27, 33, 104
domain models, 104, 110
domains, 6, 26, 30, 35, 36, 37, 39, 40, 41, 42, 45, 46, 49, 54, 59, 63, 64, 65, 66, 80, 81, 88, 90, 92, 94, 96, 100, 101, 102, 103, 104, 105, 106, 108, 110, 111, 112, 114, 117, 118, 122
  boundaries, 66
  domain-specific meaning, 105, 118
enrichment layer
  derived meaning, 27, 82
enterprise data architecture, 13, 15
enterprise semantic layer
  core entities, 25, 57
extract, transform, and load (ETL), i, 13, 15, 26, 67, 73, 78, 90, 115
feature engineering, 27, 99
federation, 79, 82, 83, 86, 87, 111, 119
governance, 12, 73, 74, 77, 80, 81, 84, 92, 97, 103, 106
governed interfaces, 26, 66, 76, 90, 92
graph databases, 31, 79
graph models, 35, 59
graphs
  edges, 37, 38, 41, 47, 51, 57, 59
  nodes, 37, 38, 41, 47, 57
heterogeneous systems, 21
identity, 10, 11, 33, 41, 64, 78
implementation patterns, 2, 72, 77, 119
  API/contract-based, 81, 82, 83, 84, 86, 87, 119
  API-based, 80
  federation and virtualization, 79, 86
  graph-based, 79, 80, 81, 82, 83, 84, 87, 111, 119
  metadata-only, 77, 78, 82, 83, 84, 85, 111
inference, 30, 79, 97
integration
  point-to-point, 13, 15, 90
integration patterns, 87
interpretation rules, 11, 22, 30
  constraints, 6, 21, 29, 30, 31, 47, 49, 73, 74, 87
  derivations, 29, 30
knowledge graphs, 2, 31, 35, 36, 37, 38, 41, 46, 99, 103
  predicate, 36, 37
  subject, 36, 37, 41, 42, 43, 73, 74
  triples, 36, 37
master data, 13, 25, 64
master data management (MDM), 13, 25, 64, 100, 101
  golden records, 25, 64, 100
meaning, 1, 2, 5, 6, 9, 10, 11, 12, 13, 15, 16, 17, 18, 19, 21, 22, 25, 26, 27, 28, 29, 30, 31, 33, 34, 42, 49, 54, 59, 61, 63, 64, 65, 67, 68, 69, 70, 73, 74, 75, 77, 78, 79, 81, 84, 90, 96, 99, 101, 102, 103, 104, 111, 113, 114, 115, 116, 117, 119, 120, 121, 122
  local, 13, 26, 63, 65
  shared, 2, 10, 64, 84, 88, 96, 99, 100, 102, 103, 107, 117

stable, 25
meaning problem, 1, 119
metadata, 1, 31, 74, 77, 78, 79, 82, 83, 84, 85, 97, 111, 119
metadata layers, 1, 78, 85
metadata repositories, 31
metrics
  definitions, 30, 78, 85
naming, 10, 13, 17
ontology, 1, 6, 7, 46, 49, 56, 59, 79, 105, 109, 120
operational data, 13
operational data stores (ODS), 13
operational systems, 13, 64, 74, 90, 92, 96
physical data, 23, 33, 74, 87, 88
physical data sources, 23
physical data structures, 23, 33, 74, 87
physical systems, 22, 33, 34, 62
privacy, 73
property graphs, 35, 49
raw data, 16, 27, 30, 63, 68
reconciliation, 17, 26, 33, 64, 67, 79, 82, 85, 86, 87, 100, 101, 113, 114
reference concepts, 25
reuse, 79, 97, 120
rules, 12, 23, 26, 29, 30, 31, 33, 49, 59, 62, 74, 85, 86, 87, 120, 122
runtime, 33, 72, 73, 75, 85, 86, 87
schema registries, 2, 81, 84
schemas, 2, 15, 18, 21, 22, 26, 43, 45, 48, 51, 61, 62, 67, 77, 80, 81, 84, 87, 88, 117, 118, 119
  database, 13, 117
  physical, 75, 86
semantic architecture, 23, 63, 72, 73, 74, 84, 110, 115, 119
  evolution, 11, 105, 107
  patterns, 2, 89, 99, 109
semantic capabilities, 23, 33, 72
semantic data layers, 1, 2, 11, 12, 16, 21, 22, 23, 25, 26, 28, 29, 30, 31, 33, 34, 35, 62, 64, 65, 66, 67, 70, 71, 72, 75, 76, 78, 80, 81, 82, 83, 86, 87, 88, 89, 90, 92, 94, 96, 99, 100, 101, 102, 105, 106, 107, 109, 111, 114, 115, 117, 120, 122
semantic data models, 35, 39, 56
semantic drift, 15, 81
semantic foundation, 17, 19, 28, 63, 66, 70, 90, 101, 103, 108
semantic inconsistency, 74, 100, 113
semantic infrastructure, 2, 99, 103
semantic interfaces, 34, 69, 76, 79, 80
semantic layer engineer, 87, 88
semantic layers
  access interface, 34
  consumption layer, 27, 28, 69, 74, 75, 76, 82, 92, 94, 103, 104, 119
  domain layer, 64, 65, 66, 92, 94, 96, 103, 104
  enrichment layer, 27, 68, 69, 76, 82, 104
  enterprise or core layer, 25, 63, 64, 65, 70, 81, 99, 100, 103, 104, 105
  implementation components, 84
  integration layer, 26, 67, 76, 79, 82, 100, 103, 104
  types, 2
semantic mapping, 26, 67, 68, 100, 104
semantic mediation, 22, 23, 33, 79, 84, 86
semantic model, 1, 7, 22, 23, 28, 29, 30, 31, 33, 34, 36, 45, 46, 47, 49, 51, 52, 53, 55, 61, 62, 74, 75, 79, 81, 84, 85, 88, 99, 101, 104, 105,

106, 107, 110, 112, 117, 118, 119, 120, 122
concepts, 2, 6, 7, 22, 23, 25, 26, 28, 29, 30, 31, 33, 35, 36, 37, 46, 56, 59, 63, 65, 66, 71, 75, 85, 86, 100, 101, 103, 104, 105, 107, 109, 111, 114, 115, 117, 119, 120, 122
definitions, 2, 7, 10, 11, 13, 17, 22, 25, 28, 30, 31, 46, 47, 48, 50, 51, 55, 57, 59, 64, 65, 66, 69, 70, 75, 78, 79, 86, 87, 100, 102, 113, 114, 115, 116, 117, 118, 122
entities, 25, 29, 40, 41, 43, 46, 53, 56, 57, 59, 63, 64, 87, 122
management, 84, 85
properties, 28, 30, 31, 35, 38, 41, 43, 49, 50, 51, 52, 53, 54, 55, 57, 59, 64, 66, 74, 79, 87, 122
relationships, 2, 6, 7, 9, 21, 22, 28, 29, 31, 35, 36, 37, 38, 41, 42, 43, 46, 48, 50, 51, 52, 53, 54, 55, 56, 57, 59, 64, 66, 80, 87, 100, 101, 117, 119, 120, 122
shared, 74, 75, 81, 119
semantic modeling, 1, 35, 36, 45, 46, 105, 117
entity analysis, 51, 53, 59
properties analysis, 41, 51, 59
relationship analysis, 41, 43, 46, 51, 59
taxonomy analysis, 51, 52, 53, 54, 57, 59
terminology analysis, 45, 46, 54, 59
semantic processing, 33
semantic queries, 33
semantic services, 85, 87
semantic stores, 31
semantic translation, 30, 115
semantics, 1, 6, 9, 10, 12, 17, 28, 57, 69, 72, 77, 79, 80, 83, 84, 85, 90, 94, 96, 97, 99, 103, 108, 113, 119, 120
software as a service (SaaS), 13, 18
source systems, 15, 19, 22, 62, 67, 68, 76
stewardship, 12
syntax, 5
taxonomy, 1, 6, 7, 51, 52, 53, 54, 55, 56, 57, 59, 79, 105, 109, 122
property, 55
relationship, 55
technical debt, 3, 13, 15
terminology, 33, 45, 46, 53, 54, 57, 59, 118
transformation logic, 67, 115
translation, 1, 17, 33, 74, 75, 79, 84, 85, 86, 87
tribal knowledge, 9, 11, 113
trust in data, 12, 72, 106
use cases, 10, 12, 28, 30, 31, 39, 59, 79, 82, 83, 110, 112, 115, 120
vehicle rental example, 36, 37, 40, 42, 46, 48, 54, 55, 59
versioning, 31, 73, 97, 106
vocabulary, 10, 18, 19, 23, 26, 34, 45, 74, 96, 99, 118
local, 105

www.ingramcontent.com/pod-product-compliance
Lightning Source LLC
LaVergne TN
LVHW022228200926
848481LV00006B/2180
* 9 7 9 8 8 9 8 1 6 1 6 2 0 *